4.50

THE CORN IS GREEN

68558 ✓

THE DRAMA LIBRARY

General Editor: EDWARD THOMPSON

THE
CORN IS GREEN

A Comedy in Three Acts

by

EMLYN WILLIAMS

HEINEMANN EDUCATIONAL BOOKS

Heinemann Educational Books Ltd
Halley Court, Jordan Hill, Oxford OX2 8EJ

OXFORD LONDON EDINBURGH
MADRID ATHENS BOLOGNA PARIS
MELBOURNE SYDNEY AUCKLAND SINGAPORE TOKYO
IBADAN NAIROBI HARARE GABORONE
PORTSMOUTH NH (USA)

ISBN 0 435 20946 9

The performing rights of this play are fully protected, and
permission to perform it, whether by amateur or profess-
ional companies, must be obtained in advance from the
Author's sole agents in England: Margery Vosper, Ltd,
8/26 Charing Cross Rd, London WC2

Printed and bound in Great Britain by
Athenaeum Press Ltd, Newcastle upon Tyne

To
S. G. C.

THE CHARACTERS
(*In the order of their appearance*)

Mr. John Goronwy Jones
Miss Ronberry
Idwal Morris
Sarah Pugh
A Groom
The Squire
Bessie Watty
Mrs. Watty
Miss Moffat
Robbart Robbatch
Glyn Thomas
Will Hughes
John Owen
Morgan Evans
Old Tom
Boys, Girls and Parents

The action of the play takes place in the living-room of a house in Glansarno, a small village in a remote Welsh countryside.

The time is the latter part of the last century, and covers a period of three years.

Act I

Scene I.   *An afternoon in June.*
Scene II.   *A night in August, six weeks later.*

Act II

Scene I.   *An early evening in August, two years later.*
Scene II.   *A morning in November, three months later.*

Act III

An afternoon in July, seven months later.

The Corn is Green was first presented in London by Stephen Mitchell at the Duchess Theatre on September 20th, 1938, with the following cast:

Mr. John Goronwy Jones	JOHN GLYN-JONES
Miss Ronberry	CHRISTINE SILVER
Idwal Morris	WILLIAM JOHN DAVIES
Sarah Pugh	DOROTHY LANGLEY
A Groom	ALBERT BIDDISCOMB
The Squire	FREDERICK LLOYD
Bessie Watty	BETTY JARDINE
Mrs. Watty	KATHLEEN HARRISON
Miss Moffat	SYBIL THORNDIKE
Robbart Robbatch	KENNETH EVANS
Glyn Thomas	WYNFORD MORSE
Will Hughes	JACK GLYN
John Owen	GLAN WILLIAMS
Morgan Evans	EMLYN WILLIAMS
Old Tom	FRANK DUNLOP

The play produced by THE AUTHOR

———

Setting and Costumes by MICHAEL WEIGHT.

ACT I

SCENE I

*The living-room of a house in Glansarno, a small village in a remote
Welsh countryside. A sunny afternoon in June, in the latter part
of the last century.*

*The house is old, and the ceiling slants away from the audience.
Facing the audience, on the right (throughout the play, "left" and
"right" refer to the audience's left and right), narrow stairs lead
up to a landing and then on the right to a passage to the bedrooms;
we can just see, facing, the door of one bedroom which is later to
be MISS MOFFAT'S. Under the landing, a low door leads to the
kitchen; at the foot of the stairs, an alcove and a door lead to a
little room which is later the study. In the back wall, to the left,
the front door, with outside it a small stone porch faintly overgrown
with ivy, and opening to the left on to a path; in the back wall, to
the right, one step leads up to a large bay window with a seat round
the recess. In the left wall, downstage, the garden door, with above
it a small side window; when the door is open we can just see a
trellised porch with a creeper. Through the thickish muslin curtains
over the bay window we glimpse a jagged stone wall and the sky.*

*The floor is of stone flags, with two rugs, one in front of the
sofa next the footlights, to mark the fireplace. Faded sprigged
wallpaper.*

*The furniture is a curious jumble of old Welsh and Victorian
pieces. A large serviceable flat-topped desk under the side window,
a desk-chair in front of it; a round table with a small chair, near
the middle of the room; an armchair, between the desk and the
table; a sofa, downstage, between the table and the foot of the
stairs; in the right wall, above the kitchen door, an old Welsh
dresser with plates and crockery; in the right wall, against the
staircase, a settle; in the window recess, a small table; below the
bay window, an old spinning-wheel. In the back wall, to the left*

I

of the front door, a small grandfather's clock. An oil lamp on the centre table, another on the desk.

The most distinctive feature of the room is the number of books on the walls, of all sorts and sizes: some in open bookcases, others on newly-built shelves, on practically every available space.

The kitchen door is open; there are books on the window seat, several on the edge of the sofa.

As the curtain rises, MR. JOHN GORONWY JONES *and* MISS RONBERRY *are arranging the last books in their places; she is sitting on a tiny stool taking books out of a large packing-case and fitting them on to narrow shelves between the garden door and the side window, flicking each one mechanically with a tiny lace handkerchief. She is a gentlewoman in her thirties, with the sort of pinched prettiness that tends to look sharp before that age, especially when it makes sporadic attempts at coquetry; she wears a hat. He is a shabby Welshman of forty, bespectacled, gloomy and intense; a volcano, harmless even in full eruption. He is perched on top of a step-ladder, arranging books on a high shelf between the front door and the bay window, dusting them vigorously before putting them in place.*

MR. JONES (*singing in a resentful bass*):

". . . Pechadur wyf, y dua'n fyw—'O Uffern!' yw fy nghri;
Gostwng dy glust, a'm llefain clyw . . .

(*Booming to a final note.*)

So—so—so—la—so—so!"

MISS RONBERRY: Your voice has given me an agonising headache. And if you must indulge in music, will you please not do it in Welsh?

MR. JONES: I wasn't indulgin' in music, I was singin' a hymn. (*Putting the last book on the shelf and climbing down.*) And if a hymn gives you a headache, there is nothing wrong with the hymn, there is something wrong with your head.

His accent is marked, but not exaggerated.

MISS RONBERRY: I still don't see the necessity for it.

MR. JONES (*picking up the empty packing-case and moving towards the kitchen*): I sing to cheer myself up.

MISS RONBERRY: What do the words mean?

2

MR. JONES: "The wicked shall burn in hell."

He goes into the kitchen. MISS RONBERRY *looks depressed, fits in the last of her books, and crosses to the books on the back of the sofa, as* IDWAL MORRIS *comes in from the garden, carrying a bunch of flowers. He is a thin, ragged boy of thirteen, very timid.*

MISS RONBERRY (*graciously, flicking the books one by one*): Is the garden nice and ready?

IDWAL: 'Sgwelwchi'n dda, d'wi'di torri'r bloda.

MISS RONBERRY (*calling*): Translation!

MR. JONES *returns from the kitchen, slowly climbs the ladder again, and settles to his books once more.*

IDWAL (*to him, as he does so*): Os gwelwchi'n dda, Mistar Jones, d'wi'di torri'r bloda, a mae'r domen yn hogla'n ofnadwy.

MR. JONES (*to* MISS RONBERRY): He says he cut the sweet peas and the rubbish-heap is smelling terrible.

MISS RONBERRY: Oh dear . . . (*Taking the flowers from* IDWAL, *and crossing to the desk with them and the books.*) His father must put something on it.

MR. JONES: That's the English all over. The devil is there, is he? Don't take him away, put a bit of scent on him! (*To* IDWAL.) Gofyn i dy dad i roi rwbeth arno am heddyw.

IDWAL: Diolch, syr.

He runs into the kitchen.

MISS RONBERRY (*arranging the sweet peas in a vase on the desk*): I hope he will have the sense to give the message.

MR. JONES: It is terrible, isn't it, the people on these green fields and flowery hillsides bein' turned out of Heaven because they cannot answer Saint Peter when he asks them who they are in English? It is wicked, isn't it, the Welsh children not bein' *born* knowing English, isn't it? (*In a crescendo of ironic mimicry.*) Good heavens, God bless my soul, by Jove, this that and the other!

MISS RONBERRY: Anybody in Wales will tell you that the people in this part of the countryside are practically barbarians. Not a single caller for fifteen miles, and even then——

SARAH PUGH *comes out of the bedroom and down the stairs.*

She is a buxom peasant-woman, with a strong Welsh accent.

SARAH: Please, miss, I made the bed lovely. And I dust——

MISS RONBERRY: That will be all, dear, the Colonel is bound to have his own manservant.

SARAH (*disappointed, going to the front door*): Then I bettar have another sit down in my post-office.

MR. JONES (*sternly*): What is the matter with your post-office?

SARAH (*turning at the door*): It has not had a letter for seven weeks. Nobody but me can write, and no good *me* writin', because nobody but me can read. If I get a telegram I put him in the window and I die straight off.

She goes.

MISS RONBERRY: You see? I can't *think* why a Colonel should elect to come and live in this place. (*Patting the last flower into position.*) There . . . (*Coming into the middle of the room, and surveying it.*) I have never *seen* so many books! I do hope the curtains will not be too feminine. (*Sitting on the sofa.*) I chose them with such care——

MR. JONES (*darkly*): Why are you taking so much trouble getting somebody else's house ready for them?

MISS RONBERRY (*flustered*): You need not have helped me if you did not wish! . . . (*Finishing sewing a rent in a cushion on the sofa.*) I am frightened of the spinning-wheel, too, and the china; his own furniture is *so* distinctive. The desk. And the waste-paper-basket. So . . . so virile.

MR. JONES: Are you hoping that the Colonel will live up to his waste-paper basket?

MISS RONBERRY: That is horrid.

MR. JONES: And then you will have two on a string: him and the Squire——

MISS RONBERRY (*pleasurably shocked*): Mr. Jones——!

MR. JONES (*implacable*): And if I was a bit more of a masher, there would be three. Worldly things, that is your trouble. "Please, Mistar Jones, my life is as empty as a rotten nutshell, so get me a husband before it is too late, double quick!"

He has gone too far.

MISS RONBERRY: You insulting man——

4

A knock at the front door; it opens and a liveried GROOM *appears.*

THE GROOM (*announcing*): The Squire.

THE SQUIRE *follows him. He is a handsome English country gentleman in his forties, wearing knickerbockers and gaiters; a hard drinker, very moustached, bluff, kind, immensely vain; and, when the time comes, obtusely obstinate.* THE GROOM *goes out again and shuts the door.*

MISS RONBERRY (*fluttering eagerly into a handshake*): Squire . . .

THE SQUIRE (*with exuberant patronage, throwing his hat on the table*): Delicious lady, delicious surprise, and a merry afternoon to ye, as our forebears put it . . . (*A cold nod.*) How are you, Jones, making the most of your half-day?

MR. JONES (*sullenly, making an uncertain effort to rise from the ladder*): Good afternoon, sir——

THE SQUIRE: Squat, dear fellow, squat, no ceremony with me! . . . (*Bowing* MISS RONBERRY *on to the sofa, and sinking himself into the armchair.*) And why, dear lady, were you not at the Travers-Ellis wedding?

MISS RONBERRY (*dashed*): Naughty! I sat next to you at the breakfast.

THE SQUIRE: By Jingo, so you did! Deuced fine breakfast . . .

MR. JONES: Excuse me——

He goes into the study, carrying the step-ladder.

MISS RONBERRY: We had a talk about children.

THE SQUIRE: *Did* we? . . . Well, the next wedding we're at, there'll be *no* chance of my forgettin' you, eh?

MISS RONBERRY: (*breath suspended, for a second*) Why?

THE SQUIRE: Because you'll be the stunning, blushing bride!

MISS RONBERRY: And who—will be the——?

THE SQUIRE (*in a paroxysm of joviality*): Now that's what *I* want to know, because *I*'m going to give you away!

MISS RONBERRY: Oh!

MR. JONES *returns from the study.*

THE SQUIRE: Now who's it going to be?

MISS RONBERRY: Squire, you are too impatient! (*Teasing.*) I am taking my time!

She laughs, catches the gleam of MR. JONES' *spectacles, and subsides quickly.* MR. JONES *sits at the table in the window seat and dusts the books there.*

THE SQUIRE: Too bad . . . No sign of the new inhabitant?

MISS RONBERRY (*sewing*): Any moment now, I think! The pony and trap met the London train at a quarter to twelve!

THE SQUIRE: Hasn't the fellow got his own private conveyance?

MISS RONBERRY: I think not.

THE SQUIRE: I hope he's all right.

MISS RONBERRY: He wrote very civilly to Mr. Jones about the house——

THE SQUIRE: Oh yes. Not a club, I remember, but not bad texture. (*Suspiciously.*) Funny sort of chap, though, eh?

MISS RONBERRY: Why?

THE SQUIRE: All these books.

A timid knock at the front door. IDWAL *enters, very frightened.*

IDWAL (*to the* SQUIRE): Os gwelwchi'n dda, syr, mae Mistar Tomos wedi 'ngyrru i yma ich gweld chi!

THE SQUIRE (*chuckling good-humouredly*): Y'know, it's as bad as being abroad . . . been among it half my life, and never get used to it.

MR. JONES (*rising, and coming down*): The groom told him, sir. that you wanted to see him.

THE SQUIRE: Oh yes—well, come here where I can see you, eh? . . . (*As* IDWAL *advances fearfully round his chair.*) Now, boy, how old are you, or whatever the Chinese is for it?

MR. JONES: Just turned thirteen, sir.

THE SQUIRE: Thirteen? Well, why aren't you working in the mine over in the next valley? Don't like to see young fellows wasting their time, y'know.

MR. JONES: He has got one lung funny.

THE SQUIRE: Oh, I see . . . Rough luck—here, laddy, there's a penny for you, and remember all work and no play makes Taffy a dull boy!

IDWAL (*delighted, going*): Diolch yn fawr, syr——

THE SQUIRE: And tell your uncle I want Ranger shod——

IDWAL (*going*): Diolch, syr——

6

THE SQUIRE: And a window mended——

IDWAL: Diolch yn fawr, syr——

He runs out by the front door.

MISS RONBERRY: But he hasn't understood your orders!

THE SQUIRE: Neither he has——

MR. JONES: He thought the Squire was havin' a chat. (*Going towards the window.*) I will tell his uncle——-

IDWAL (*calling shrilly to his friends, in the road*): Tomos—Aneurin—dyma'r cerbyd—dewch i wel'd—fe ddwedai wrth y Scweiar—brysiwch!

MISS RONBERRY (*rising, excited*): That must be something——

IDWAL *appears at the front door, panting with expectation.*

IDWAL (*to the* SQUIRE): Pliss, syr, dyma'r cerbyd!

He darts back, leaving the door open.

MISS RONBERRY: He must mean the Colonel—how gratifying——

THE SQUIRE: Capital——

He rises and stands between the armchair and the garden door, while MR. JONES *shrinks back into the window-recess, as* BESSIE WATTY *wanders shyly in from the front door. She is an extremely pretty, plump little girl of fourteen; it is a moment before one realises that her demureness is too good to be true. She wears her hair over her shoulders, is dressed very plainly, in a shabby sailor suit and hat, and carries brown-paper parcels. She stands immobile near the table. She is followed by* MRS. WATTY, *a middle-aged Cockney servant, dressed for travelling, carrying a hamper in her arms surmounted by several articles tied together with rope, including a kettle, a rolling-pin, and a pudding-basin. Her self-confidence is not so overwhelming as the* SQUIRE'S, *but it is quite as complete and as kindly. She looks round uncertainly, unable to dispose of her burden.*

MRS. WATTY (*to the* SQUIRE): D'you speak English?

THE SQUIRE (*taken aback*): I do.

MRS. WATTY: Be a dear an' 'old this!

She hands him the hamper, takes the rest, manœuvres them on to the table, and hurries out through the front door.

THE SQUIRE: Crikey! A Colonel with an abigail! (*Catching*

BESSIE's *owl-like expression, and stopping short.*) Why don't *you* say something?

BESSIE: I never speak till I'm spoken to.

THE SQUIRE: Oh . . . Well, who was that?

BESSIE: My mummy. I never had no daddy.

> *Her accent is not as natural as her mother's; she sometimes strains to be ladylike, especially at moments like this.* MRS. WATTY *returns carrying two large cloth-covered parcels.*

MRS. WATTY: My Gawd, they're heavy.

MISS RONBERRY: What are they?

MRS. WATTY: Books.

> *She drops the parcels on the floor, takes the hamper from the* SQUIRE, *and places it on the table.*

THE SQUIRE: Is your employer with you, my good woman?

MRS. WATTY: No, followed be'ind, most of the way. (*Hurrying back to the front door and peering down the street.*) Ought to be 'ere by now, I'll 'ave a see . . . (*Calling.*) 'Ere we are! Tally-o! Thought we'd lost you!

> *A pause.* MISS MOFFAT *comes in from the road, wheeling a bicycle. She is about forty, a healthy Englishwoman with an honest face, clear, beautiful eyes, a humorous mouth, a direct friendly manner, and unbounded vitality, which is prevented from tiring the spectator by its capacity for sudden silences and for listening. Her most prominent characteristic is her complete unsentimentality. She wears a straw hat, collar and tie, and a dark unexaggerated skirt; a satchel hangs from her shoulder.*

MISS MOFFAT: I was hoping to pass you, but that last hill was too much for me. (*Displaying the bicycle.*) There's a smallish crowd already, so I thought I'd better bring Priscilla inside. Watty, can you find somewhere for her?

> *She gives the room a quick appraising look, peers out of the side window, and nods pleasantly at the* SQUIRE.

I think I'll have a look at the garden first.

> *She goes out into the garden. The* SQUIRE *stares at her.*

MRS WATTY (*wheeling the bicycle gingerly towards the kitchen*): Dunno, I'm sure—that must be my kitchen in there, we'll 'ave to ang 'er with the bacon. (*To* BESSIE.) Come on, girl, give us a 'and, don't stand there gettin' into mischief!

BESSIE: I'm frightened of it.

MRS. WATTY: It won't bite you! Most it can do is catch fire, and I'll 'ave a drop o' water ready for it . . .

Her voice fades away into the kitchen.

BESSIE: Has anybody got a sweetie?

MISS RONBERRY: No.

BESSIE (*depressed*): Oh . . .

She trails after her mother into the kitchen. MISS MOFFAT returns, very businesslike; not a movement of hers is wasted.

MISS MOFFAT: It's bigger than I expected . . . (*Shutting the front door, then unpinning her hat, pleasantly, as they stare at her.*) There! Good afternoon! (*Looking round the room, as she pitches her hat on to the desk.*) So this is my house . . .

THE SQUIRE (*blustering*): No, it isn't!

MISS MOFFAT: Oh? Isn't this Pengarth? The name of the building, I mean?

MISS RONBERRY: Yes, it is——

MRS. WATTY returns from the kitchen, motions to MR. JONES to unpack the books in the hamper, and takes the kettle and its appurtenances back into the kitchen. MR. JONES unpacks. During this, MISS MOFFAT speaks.

MISS MOFFAT (*relieved*): That's right, it was left me by my uncle, Doctor Moffat. I'm Miss Moffat. (*As she unstraps her satchel.*) I take it you're Miss Ronberry, who so kindly corresponded with me?

THE SQUIRE (*sternly*): But surely those letters were written by a man?

MISS MOFFAT: Well, if they were, I have been grossly deceiving myself for over forty years . . . (*Addressing him as his equal and not as his inferior, for him a new experience with women.*) Now this is jolly interesting. Why did it never occur to you that I might be a woman?

THE SQUIRE: Well—the paper wasn't scented——

MISS RONBERRY: And such a bold hand——

THE SQUIRE: And that long piece about the lease being ninety-nine years, don't you know——

9

MISS MOFFAT (*concerned*): Was there anything wrong with it?

THE SQUIRE: No, there wasn't, that's the point.

MISS MOFFAT: I see.

MISS RONBERRY: And surely you signed your name very oddly?

MISS MOFFAT: My initials, L. C. Moffat? You see, I've never felt that Lily Christabel really suited me.

MISS RONBERRY (*sitting on the sofa*): And I thought it meant Lieutenant-Colonel . . . But there *was* a military title after it!

MISS MOFFAT (*after thinking a second*): M.A., Master of Arts.

THE SQUIRE: Arts? D'ye mean the degree my father bought me when I came down from the Varsity?

MISS MOFFAT: The very same. Except that I was at Aberdeen, and had to work jolly hard for mine.

THE SQUIRE: A female M.A.? And how long's that going to last?

MISS MOFFAT (*placing her satchel next the desk*): Quite a long time, I hope, considering we've been waiting for it for two thousand years.

MR. JONES (*who has been silent as the grave, since she entered*): Are you saved?

MISS MOFFAT (*starting, turning and taking him in for the first time*): I beg your pardon?

MR. JONES: Are you Church or Chapel?

MISS MOFFAT: I really don't know . . . (*To the* SQUIRE, *as she crosses to the table to fetch some books.*) And now you know all about me, what do *you* do?

THE SQUIRE (*distantly, moving towards the front door*): I'm afraid I don't do anything.

He extricates his hat angrily from the table.

MISS RONBERRY (*shocked*): Mr. Treverby owns the Hall!

MISS MOFFAT (*frank and friendly*): Really. I've never had much to do with the landed gentry. Interesting.

THE SQUIRE (*to* MISS RONBERRY): Au revoir, dear lady. 'Day, Jones.

He goes frigidly out by the front door.

MISS MOFFAT: Well, nobody could say that I've made a conquest there. . . . (*Crossing towards the stairs.*) What's the matter with him?

MRS. WATTY *comes in from the kitchen, carrying a small tray with three cups and saucers.*

MRS. WATTY (*placing the tray on the table*): I found the tea, ma'am, it *looks* all right——

MISS MOFFAT: Good——

MRS. WATTY: An' the big luggage is comin' after——

MISS MOFFAT (*opening the study door*): This isn't a bad little room——

MR. JONES *crosses to the desk with books from the table.*

MRS. WATTY (*to the others*): Where's his lordship?

MISS MOFFAT (*going upstairs*): Took offence and left.

She disappears down the passage.

MRS. WATTY: Took offence? At 'er?

MISS RONBERRY: I am afraid so.

MRS. WATTY: I'm jiggered! (*Arranging the cups and saucers.*) What d'*you* think of 'er, eh? Ain't she a clinker?

MISS RONBERRY: She is unusual, is she not?

MRS. WATTY: She's a clinker, that's what. Terrible strong-willed, o' course, terrible. Get 'er into mischief, I keep tellin' 'er. Would bring me 'ere. I said no, I said, not with my past, I said.

MISS RONBERRY: Your past?

MRS. WATTY: Before she took me up. But what with 'er, an now I've joined the Corpse, it's all blotted out.

MR. JONES: The Corpse?

MRS. WATTY: The Militant Righteous Corpse. Ran into 'em in the street I did, singin' and prayin' and collectin', full blast; and I been a different woman since. (*Turning to* MR. JONES.) Are *you* saved?

MR. JONES (*stiffening*): Yes, I am.

MRS. WATTY: So'm I, ain't it lovely?

MISS RONBERRY: But what *was* . . . your past?

MRS. WATTY (*sorrowfully*): Light fingers.

MISS RONBERRY: Light fingers? (*The truth dawning on her.*) you mean—stealing?

MRS. WATTY: Everywhere I went. Terrible. Pennies, stockin's, brooches, spoons, tiddly, anything; and I always looked so pi!

Every time there was a do, everything went; and I always knew it was me!

> MISS MOFFAT *comes downstairs.*

(*Moving towards the kitchen.*) I was just tellin' 'em about my trouble.

MISS MOFFAT: Well, don't tell them any more. Is your kitchen all right?

MRS. WATTY: I ain't *seed* no mice yet.

> *She goes into the kitchen.* MISS MOFFAT *looks round again. Far away, softly, the sound of boys' voices, singing an old country song, in harmony, in Welsh: "Yr Hufen Melyn".*

MISS MOFFAT: I agree with the last tenant's taste. Though I don't see myself spinning very much . . . (*Warmly.*) You have arranged my things quite splendidly, Miss Ronberry, I do thank you—both of you . . . (*Savouring the atmosphere of the room.*) I like this house . . . (*As the music grows imperceptibly, in the distance.*) What's that singing?

MR. JONES: Boys coming home from the mine.

MISS RONBERRY: They burst into song on the slightest provocation. You mustn't take any notice——

MISS MOFFAT: I like it . . . (*After listening a moment, looking out of the side window.*) And those mountains. That grand wild countryside . . . the foreign-looking people . . . (*As the singing dies away.*) But business . . . I've heard about that mine. How far is it?

MR. JONES: It is the Glasynglo coal mine, six miles over the hills.

MISS MOFFAT (*moving towards the bay window*): Hm . . .

MISS RONBERRY: We're hoping it will stay the only one, or our scenery will be ruined—such a pretty landscape——

MISS MOFFAT (*looking out, suddenly*): What is the large empty building next door?

MR. JONES: Next door? The old barn belongin' to the Gwalia Farm, before the farm was burnt down——

MISS MOFFAT: So it's free?

MR. JONES (*perplexed*): Free? Yes——

MISS RONBERRY (*losing interest, rising and crossing in front of the table*): I am over-staying my welcome—so very charming——

MR. JONES (*taking the rest of the books to the desk*): I also—all the volumes are dusted——

MISS MOFFAT: I want you two people. Very specially. First you, Miss Ronberry. (*Coming down to her.*) I used to meet friends of yours at lectures in London. You live alone, you have just enough money, you're not badly educated, and time lies heavy on your hands.

MISS RONBERRY (*sitting again, suddenly, in the armchair*): The Wingroves! How mean—I should never have thought——

MISS MOFFAT: Isn't that so?

MISS RONBERRY: Not at all. When the right gentleman appears——

MISS MOFFAT: If you're a spinster well on in her thirties, he's lost his way and isn't coming. Why don't you face the fact and enjoy yourself, the same as I do?

MISS RONBERRY: But when did you give up hope—oh, what a horrid expression——

MISS MOFFAT: I can't recall ever having any hope. (*Sitting on the sofa.*) Visitors used to take a long look at my figure and say: "*She's* going to be the clever one." I shall never forget what I looked like the night my mother put me on the market. A tub with pink ribbon in every hoop. And when the only young man who had spoken to me said I was the sort of girl he'd like for a sister, then I knew.

MISS RONBERRY: But a woman's only future is to marry and—and fulfil the duties of——

MISS MOFFAT: Skittles. I'd have made a shocking wife anyway.

MISS RONBERRY: But haven't you ever—been in love?

MISS MOFFAT: No.

MISS RONBERRY: How very odd.

MISS MOFFAT: I've never talked to a man for more than five minutes without wanting to box his ears.

MR. JONES *looks apprehensive.*

MISS RONBERRY: But how have you passed your time since——

MISS MOFFAT: Since I had no hope? Very busily. In the East End, for years.

MISS RONBERRY (*politely*): Social service?

MISS MOFFAT: If you like; though there's nothing very social about washing invalids with every unmentionable ailment under the sun . . . I've read a lot, too. I'm afraid I'm what is known as an educated woman. Which brings me to Mr. Jones; (*to him*) the Wingroves told me all about you, too.

MR. JONES (*advancing stiffly*): My conscience is as clear as the snow.

MISS MOFFAT: I'm sure it is, but you're a disappointed man, aren't you?

MR. JONES (*startled*): How can I be disappointed when I am saved?

MISS MOFFAT: Oh, but you can! You can't really enjoy sitting all by yourself on a raft, on a sea containing everybody you know. You're disappointed because you're between two stools.

MR. JONES (*at a loss*): Between two stools? On a raft?

MISS MOFFAT: Exactly. Your father was a grocer with just enough money to send you to a grammar-school, with the result that you are educated beyond your sphere, and yet fail to qualify for the upper classes. You feel frustrated, and fall back on being saved. Am I right?

MR. JONES (*turning away*): It is such a terrible thing you have said that I will have to think it over.

MISS MOFFAT: Do, but in the meantime would you two like to stop moping and be very useful to me?

MISS RONBERRY: Useful?

MISS MOFFAT (*walking about*): Tell me—within a radius of five miles, how many families are there round here?

MISS RONBERRY (*at home for a moment*): Families? There's the Squire, of course, and Mrs. Gwent-Price in the little Plas Lodge, quite a dear thing——

MISS MOFFAT: I mean ordinary people.

MISS RONBERRY (*lost again*): The villagers?

MISS MOFFAT: Yes. How many families?

MISS RONBERRY: I really haven't the faint——

MR. JONES: There are about twenty families in the village and fifteen in the farms around.

MISS MOFFAT: Many children?

MR. JONES: What age?

MISS MOFFAT: Up to sixteen or seventeen.

MR. JONES: Round here they are only children till they are twelve. Then they are sent away over the hills to the mine, and in one week they are old men.

MISS MOFFAT: I see . . . How many can read or write?

MR. JONES: Next to none.

MISS RONBERRY: Why do you ask?

MISS MOFFAT: Because I am going to start a school for them.

MISS RONBERRY: Start a school for them? (*Coldly.*) What for?

MISS MOFFAT: What for? You cheerfully contribute funds to send missionaries to African heathens, who are as happy as the day is long, and you ask me what for? See these books? Hundreds of 'em, and something wonderful to read in every single one— these nippers are to be cut off from all that, for ever, are they? Why? Because they happen to be born penniless in an uncivilized countryside, coining gold down there in that stinking dungeon for some beef-headed old miser!

MR. JONES (*roused*): That's right . . .

MISS MOFFAT: The printed page, what is it? One of the miracles of all time, that's what! And yet when these poor babbies set eyes on it, they might just as well have been struck by the miracle of sudden blindness; and that, to my mind, is plain infamous!

MR. JONES (*in an excited whisper*): My goodness, Miss, that's right . . .

MISS RONBERRY: The *ordinary* children, you mean?

MISS MOFFAT: Yes, my dear, the ordinary children, that came into the world by the same process exactly as you and I. When I heard that this part of the world was a disgrace to a Christian country, I knew this house was a godsend; I am going to start a school, immediately, next door in the barn, and you are going to help me!

MISS RONBERRY: I?

15

The rest of the scene is played very quickly.

MISS MOFFAT (*settling again on the end of the sofa*): Yes, you! You're going to fling away your parasol and your kid gloves, and you're going to stain those tapering fingers with a little honest toil!

MISS RONBERRY: I couldn't teach those children, I couldn't! They—they smell!

MISS MOFFAT: If we'd never been taught to wash, so would we; we'll put 'em under the pump. . . . Mr. Jones, d'ye know what I'm going to do with that obstinate old head of yours?

MR. JONES: My head?

MISS MOFFAT: I'm going to crack it open with a skewer. And I'm going to excavate all those chunks of grammar-school knowledge, give 'em a quick dust, and put 'em to some use at last——

MR. JONES: I am a solicitor's clerk in Gwaenygam and I earn thirty-three shillings per week——

MISS MOFFAT: I'll give you thirty-four—and your lunch.

MISS RONBERRY: I have an enormous house to run, and the flowers to do——

MISS MOFFAT: Shut it up except one room, and leave the flowers to die a natural death—in their own beds. . . . (*Crossing excitedly to the foot of the stairs.*) I've been left a little money and I know exactly what I am going to do with it——

MR. JONES: But those children are in the mine—earning money —how can they——

MISS MOFFAT: I'll pay their parents the few miserable pennies they get out of it. . . . And when I've finished with you, *you* won't have time to think about snapping up a husband, and *you* won't have time to be so pleased that you're saved! Well?

MR. JONES (*after a pause, solemnly*): I do not care if you are not chapel, I am with you.

MISS MOFFAT: Good! (*Crossing swiftly to the desk, and taking her satchel.*) I have all the details worked out, I'll explain roughly . . . Come along, my dears, gather round——

She takes the dazed MISS RONBERRY *by the arm, sits her beside her on the sofa, and beckons* MR. JONES *to sit on her other side.*

(*Opening the satchel and spilling a sheaf of papers on to her knee.*) Of course we must go slowly at first, but if we put our backs into it . . . (*Aglow.*) Here we are, three stolid middle-aged folk, settled in our little groove and crammed with benefits; and *there* are those babbies scarcely out of the shell, that have no idea they are even breathing the air . . . Only God can know how their life will end, but He will give us the chance to direct them a little of the way——

MR. JONES (*intoning, seized with religious fervour*): We have the blessed opportunity to raise up the children from the bowels of the earth where the devil hath imprisoned them in the powers of darkness, and bring them to the light of knowledge——

MRS. WATTY (*coming in from the kitchen, sailing round the table with an enormous steaming teapot, calling shrilly, as* MISS MOFFAT *displays her papers*): Tea!

  Black out. The curtain falls, and rises immediately on

SCENE II

A night in August, six weeks later. The window-curtains are closed and the lamps lit. The armchair has been pushed above the desk, and a small bench put in its place, facing the audience. Red geraniums in pots across the window-sills. MISS MOFFAT'S *straw hat is slung over the knob at the foot of the stairs. The big desk, the desk-chair, the sofa and the settle are littered with books, exercise-books, and sheets of paper. Apart from these details the room is unchanged.*

  Sitting on the bench are five black-faced miners, between twelve and sixteen years of age, wearing caps, mufflers, boots and corduroys embedded in coal; they look as if they had been commanded to wait. They all look alike under their black; the ringleader is MORGAN EVANS, *fifteen, quick and impudent; his second is* ROBBART ROBBATCH, *a big, slow boy, a year or two older; the others are* GLYN THOMAS, WILL HUGHES *and* JOHN OWEN.

  MRS. WATTY *comes downstairs, carrying a basket of washing.*

MRS. WATTY (*singing*): "I'm saved, I am—I'm saved, I am—I'm S-A-V-E-D——" (*Seeing the boys, and halting.*) You 'ere again?

ROBBART (*nudging* MORGAN): Be mai'n ddeud?

MRS. WATTY: I said, you 'ere again?

MORGAN: No, miss.

MRS. WATTY: What d'ye mean, no, miss?

MORGAN (*a strong accent*): We issn't 'ere again, miss.

MRS. WATTY: What are you, then?

MORGAN: We issn't the same lot ass this mornin', miss.

MRS. WATTY (*coming downstairs*): Ain't you?

MORGAN: Miss Ronny-berry tell us to wait, miss.

MRS. WATTY (*calling*): Ma'am!

MISS MOFFAT (*in the bedroom*): Yes?

MRS. WATTY: Five more nigger-boys for you!

> *She goes into the kitchen.* MORGAN *takes a bottle from his pocket and swigs at it; one of the others holds out his hand, takes the bottle, gulps, and gives it back, while another begins to hum, absent-mindedly, a snatch of the same song as before—"Yr Hufen Melyn". The rest (including* MORGAN) *take up the harmony and sing it to the end.*

ROBBART (*loudly, derisively*): Please, miss, can I have a kiss?

MORGAN: No, you can't, you dirty Taffy, you dirty my nose!

ROBBART: Get out o' my school, you dirty Taffies——

MORGAN: Get out——

> *He gives a hefty push and sends all the others sprawling to the floor. Pandemonium, involving a torrent of Welsh imprecations:*

GLYN: Denna'r trydydd tro—be haru ti, diawl——

JOHN: Get out o' my school, cer gartra—mochyn budur gwaith glo—cer gartra——

WILL: Wtisho dy drwyn i waedu eto?

MORGAN: Sospon mawr, yn berwi ar y llawr—sospon bach—wtish dy drwyn di i waedu?

> *In the middle of this* MRS. WATTY *comes in from the kitchen, her arms covered in soapsuds.*

MRS. WATTY: Now, now, you boys, me on me washin' night too!

MORGAN: Please, miss, can I have a kiss?

MRS. WATTY (*shocked*): You naughty boy! You wait till

you see Miss Moffat, she'll give you what for!   (*On her way back to the kitchen.*) Can I 'ave a kiss, indeed, bad as the West End . . .

> *She goes.*

ROBBART (*bored, singing raucously*): "Boys and girls come out to play——"

> *He claps his hands to his knees, the others half take up the refrain.*
> MR. JONES *comes in from the front door.*

MORGAN: Sh!

> *The boys are silent, turn, and watch* MR. JONES. *He eyes them fearfully.*

MORGAN (*blandly*): Good evenin', sir.

MR. JONES (*relieved, taking off his hat*): Good evening.

> *He moves towards the kitchen.*

MORGAN (*suddenly*): I seed you and the lady teacher be'ind the door!

> *A chorus of* "Oooo!" *in mock horror from him and the others.*

MR. JONES (*frightened and dignified*): You wait till you see Miss Moffat. She will give you what for.

MORGAN (*muttering, mimicking him*): You wait till you see Miss Moffat, she will give you what for!

> *The others join in as* MR. JONES *goes into the kitchen:* "You wait till you see Miss Moffat, she will give you what for!"

MORGAN: Shh!

> *The rest are silent, as* MISS MOFFAT *comes downstairs from the bedroom. She is dressed much the same, and carries a roll of papers.*

MISS MOFFAT (*calling*): I told you, the shape of the bedroom doesn't allow for a door into the barn—oh, she isn't here . . . (*Picking up her hat from the knob and putting it on.*) Sorry to keep you waiting, boys, but I have to go across to Mr. Rees, the carpenter, and then I'll be able to talk to you. In the meantime, will you go to the pump in the garden shed, and wash your hands. Through there. You'll find a lantern.

> *They stare before them, immovable.*

(*Smiling.*) Did you understand all that?

MORGAN (*with false submissiveness*): Yes, miss.

THE OTHERS (*taking his tone*): Thank you, miss.

MISS MOFFAT: Good.

MORGAN (*as she starts for the front door, loud and shrill*): Please, miss, can I have a kiss?

> *A pause.*

MISS MOFFAT (*turning*): What did you say?

MORGAN (*rising, leaping over the bench, and grinning at the others*): Please, miss, can I have a kiss?

MISS MOFFAT (*after a pause, quietly*): Of course you can.

> *She walks briskly down, puts one foot on the end of the bench, seizes* MORGAN, *turns him over on her knee, spanks him six times, hard, with the roll of papers, then releases him.*

(*Looking coolly at the others.*) Can I oblige anybody else?

> *She goes out by the front door. The others follow her with their eyes, aghast, in silence.*

ROBBART (*imitating* MORGAN): Please, miss, can I 'ave a smack bottom?

> *An uproar of mirth, and a quick tangle of Welsh.*

MORGAN: Cythral uffarn——

GLYN: Be hari hi—hi a'i molchi——

JOHN: Pwy sisho molchi——

WILL: Welso ti'rioed wraig fel ene——

MORGAN: Mae'n lwcus na ddaru mi mo'i thrawo hi lawr a'i lladd hi——

ROBBART: Nawn i drio molchi—dewch hogia—mae'n well nag eistedd yma—dewch——

> *They lumber into the garden,* MORGAN *muttering furiously, the others talking and laughing. Their voices die away.* MR. JONES'S *head appears timidly round from the kitchen. He sees they are gone, gives a sigh of relief, and comes into the room, carrying books. He sits at the desk, intoning a hymn.* BESSIE *comes in from the front door, dejected and sulky. She is munching a sweet; her hair is in curls, and one curl is turned round one finger, which she holds stiffly in the air. She lays her hat on the sofa, then decides* MR. JONES'S *company is better than none.*

BESSIE: Would you like a sweetie?

MR. JONES: No thank you, my little dear. Have you had another walk?

BESSIE: Yes, Mr. Jones. (*Perching on the edge of the sofa.*) All by myself.

MR. JONES (*genially, for him*): Did you see anybody?

BESSIE: Only a lady and a gentleman in the lane, and mother told me never to look . . . (*As he pretends not to have heard.*) I do miss the shops. London's full o' them, you know.

MR. JONES: Full of fancy rubbish, you mean.

BESSIE: I'd like to be always shoppin', I would. Sundays and all . . . Mr. Jones, d'you remember sayin' everybody who don't go to chapel on Sundays will go to hell?

MR. JONES (*bravely*): Indeed I do.

BESSIE: Last Sunday Miss Moffat was diggin' the garden all afternoon; she's in for it, then, isn't she?

MR. JONES: Miss Moffat is a good woman. If she went to chapel she would be a better one, but she is still a good woman.

MRS. WATTY (*calling, in the kitchen*): Bessie!

BESSIE (*slyly*): Mr. Jones, is it true the school idea isn't going on that well?

MR. JONES (*after a pause*): Who told you that?

BESSIE: Miss Ronberry was sayin' something to my mum— oh, I wasn't listenin'! . . . Besides, we've been here six weeks, and nothin's started yet.

MR. JONES: Everything is splendid.

BESSIE (*disappointed*): Oh, I am glad. Miss Moffat's been cruel to me, but I don't bear no grudge.

MR. JONES: Cruel to you?

BESSIE: She hides my sweets. (*Going.*) She's a liar too.

MR. JONES: A liar?

BESSIE: Told me they're bad for me, and it says on the bag they're nourishin' . . . (*Going, dipping her nose into her bag.*) And the idea of learnin' school with those children, ooh . . .

MR. JONES: Why are you holding your hair like that?

BESSIE: These are me curls. D'you think it's nice?

MR. JONES: It is nice, but it is wrong.

MRS. WATTY (*calling shrilly, in the kitchen*): Bess-ie!

BESSIE: I've been curlin' each one round me finger and holdin'

it tight till it was all right. (*Moving, dejectedly, still holding her hair.*
My finger's achin' something terrible.

She goes into the kitchen. A knock at the front door.

Mr. Jones (*calling*): Dewch ifewn.

*IDWAL appears, drawing a small wooden crate on tiny wheels
which he pushes to the front of the sofa. Miss Ronberry comes
in from the study, poring over a book and looking harassed.*

IDWAL: Cloch yr ysgol, Mistar Jones.

Mr. Jones: Diolch, ymachgeni. Nosdawch.

IDWAL: Nosdawch, Mistar Jones.

*He goes back through the front door. Miss Ronberry sits on
the settle.*

Miss Ronberry: It says here that eight sevens are fifty-six.
Then it says that seven eights are fifty-six—I can't see that at all.

*Miss Moffat returns from the front door. Her cheerfulness
is a little forced.*

Well?

Miss Moffat: No good.

Miss Ronberry: Oh dear.

Miss Moffat (*throwing down her hat*): Mr. Rees says he's had
a strict order not to discuss lining the roof till the lease of the
barn is signed.

Mr. Jones: Who gave the order?

Miss Moffat: That's what I want to know?

Miss Ronberry: And when will the lease be signed?

Miss Moffat: Never, it seems to me. (*Anxiously, to* Mr.
Jones.) Did you call at the solicitor's?

Mr. Jones (*unwillingly*): They have located Sir Herbert Vezey,
but he is now doubtful about letting the barn and will give his
decision by post.

Miss Moffat: But why? He'd already said it was no use to
him. And my references were impeccable . . . (*Flinging herself
on the sofa, on top of papers and books.*) Why?

Miss Ronberry: You look tired.

Miss Moffat: It's been a bit of a day. A letter from the
mine to say no child can be released above ground—that's all
blethers, but still . . . A request from the public house not to

start a school in case it interferes with beer-swilling and games of chance. A message from the chapel people to the effect that I am a foreign adventuress with cloven feet; and Priscilla's got a puncture. A bit of a day.

MRS. WATTY *comes in from the kitchen, carrying a cup of tea.*

MRS. WATTY: Drop o' tea, ma'am, I expect you've 'ad a bit of a day . . .

MISS MOFFAT: Who was that at the back, anything important?

MRS. WATTY: (*handing* MISS MOFFAT *her tea, and stirring it for her*): Only the person that does for that Mrs. Gwent-Price. Would you not 'ave your school opposite her lady because of her lady's 'eadaches.

MISS MOFFAT (*angry*): What did you say?

MRS. WATT: I pulverised 'er. (*Stirring, hard.*) I said it would be a shame, I said, if there was such a shindy over the way that the village couldn't hear Mrs. Double-Barrel givin' her 'usband what for, I said. The person didn't know where to put 'erself.

She goes back into the kitchen.

MR. JONES (*gathering books and making to cross towards the study*): That has not helped the peace in the community, neither.

MISS MOFFAT: I know, but she does make a tip-top cup of tea. . . . (*Seeing the crate, wearily.*) What's that?

MR. JONES: It is the bell, for the school.

MISS MOFFAT (*sitting up, more cheerful*): Oh, is it?

MISS RONBERRY (*rising*): The bell? Do let us have a peep——

MISS MOFFAT *unhinges the side of the crate and shows the bell.*

It is an old one, about a cubic foot in size.

MR. JONES: It was on Llantalon Monastery before it burnt down——

MISS MOFFAT: Look, it's got the rope, and everything . . . (*Getting depressed again.*) Well, it's good to see it, anyway.

MISS RONBERRY: The mason finished the little tower for it yesterday—do let us tell those boys to put it up! It'll bring us luck!

MISS MOFFAT (*sitting on the sofa drinking her tea*): If it keeps them out of mischief till I'm ready——

MISS RONBERRY: Mr. Jones, do go and tell them!

MR. JONES giving her a doubtful look and goes towards the garden. A sudden noise of raucous abuse outside in the shed; he winces, and goes.

MISS MOFFAT: Poor Jonesy, he's terrified of 'em.

MISS RONBERRY: So am I. They're so big. And so black——

A knock at the front door. SARAH runs in, excited, leaving the door open behind her.

SARAH: A letter from a gentleman that own the barn, I had a good look at the seal!

MISS MOFFAT: At last——

She hands her cup to MISS RONBERRY, takes the letter quickly from SARAH and reads it.

MISS RONBERRY (*putting the cup on the settle*): What does it say?

MISS MOFFAT: Sir Herbert still cannot give a definite decision until the seventeenth. (*Crushing the letter.*) Another week wasted. This is infuriating.

She rises and crosses towards the desk.

MISS RONBERRY: Does it mean he may not let you have it?

SARAH (*disappointed*): Oh . . .

She moves towards the front door.

MISS MOFFAT: He must—it would ruin everything——

MISS RONBERRY: Sarah, isn't there another empty building *anywhere* round here?

SARAH (*considering*): There is the pigstyes on the Maes Road, but they issn't big enough.

She goes. MISS MOFFAT sits in the desk chair.

MISS RONBERRY: Can't we start afresh somewhere else?

MISS MOFFAT: I've spent too much on preparations here—besides, I felt so right here from the start—I *can't* leave now. . . . I'm a Christian woman, but I could smack Sir Herbert's face till my arm dropped off.

The front door is opened unceremoniously and the SQUIRE strides in; he is in full evening dress, without a hat, and smokes a cigar; he is a little flushed with port. He smiles foolishly at MISS MOFFAT.

THE SQUIRE: Jolly good evenin', teacher. Remember me?

MISS MOFFAT: Would you mind going outside, knocking, and waiting quite a long time before I say "Come in"?

THE SQUIRE: Jolly good! Parlour games, what?

MISS RONBERRY (*horrified*): But Miss Moffat, it's the *Squire!* Squire, you must forget you ever saw me in this dress—so ashamed—I shan't be a moment——

She runs upstairs into the bedroom.

THE SQUIRE: Rat tat tat, one two three four come in, one two three four, forward *march!* My dear madam, you're not in class now!

A knock at the garden door.

Come in!

ROBBART enters. His attitude is a little chastened, though he does not see the SQUIRE. He is followed by MR. JONES and MORGAN, who carries a lantern.

ROBBART (*touching his forelock*): Please Miss, for the bell.

THE SQUIRE (*with jolly patronage*): Evening, Jones! Evening, boys!

The boys recognise him, and doff their caps, deeply impressed.

(*With mock solemnity.*) I am appalled to observe, my boys, that you are still soiling your fingers in that disgusting coal-mine!

An awkward pause.

MR. JONES: Excuse me, please . . .

He goes into the study. ROBBART makes an uncertain movement towards the bell.

THE SQUIRE: What's that you've got there?

ROBBART: Bell, syr, for the school.

THE SQUIRE (*laughing loudly*): Up with it, boys, up with it!

ROBBART lifts the crate and carries it out of the front door, which MORGAN has opened for him. MORGAN follows him, shutting the door.

THE SQUIRE (*during this*): Ding dong bell—teacher's in the well! . : . (*Pushing books off the sofa and sitting on it.*) Now, my dear madam——

MISS MOFFAT: I'm rather irritable this evening, so unless there's a reason for your visit——

THE SQUIRE: Oh, but there is! Very important message. Word of mouth. From a gent that's just been dining with me. Sir Herbert Vezey.

MISS MOFFAT (*with a start*): Yes? . . . Oh, do be quick . . . !

THE SQUIRE: He has definitely decided that he has no use for the barn—but . . . (*Rising and lifting a finger, playfully.*) . . . he does not see it as a school, and under no circumstances will he let it as such, so he must regretfully decline, et cetera.

> *He sits down suddenly. A pause.* MISS MOFFAT *tries in vain to hide her chagrin.*

MISS MOFFAT: He implied in his first letter that he would be willing to sell.

THE SQUIRE: Then some big wig must have made him change his mind, mustn't he?

MISS MOFFAT (*suddenly looking at him, incredulously*): You?

THE SQUIRE (*rising, serious, and taking the floor with a certain authority*): I have not called on you, madam, because I have been eyeing your activities very closely from afar—— (*Confused.*) It is with dis—disapproval and—er—dis——

MISS MOFFAT: It is unwise to embark on a speech with the vocabulary of a child of five.

THE SQUIRE (*suddenly aggressive*): I am not going to have any of this damned hanky-panky in my village!

MISS MOFFAT: *Your* village?

THE SQUIRE: *My* village! I am no braggart, but I'd have you know that everything you can see from that window—and you haven't got a bad view—*I own!* (*Heavily.*) Now, my dear madam——

MISS MOFFAT (*in an outburst*): And stop calling me your dear madam, I'm not married, I'm not French, and you haven't the slightest affection for me!

THE SQUIRE: Oh . . . First of all, I'm not one to hit a woman below the belt. If you know what I mean. Always be fair—to the fair sex. . . . All my life I've done my level best for the villagers—they call me Squire, y'know, term of affection, jolly touching—I mean, a hamper every Christmas, the whole shoot, and a whopping tankard of beer on my birthday, and on my twenty-firster they all got a mug——

MISS MOFFAT: Go on.

THE SQUIRE: They jabber away in that funny lingo, but bless

their hearts, it's a free country! But puttin' 'em up to read English, and pothooks, and givin' 'em ideas—if there were more people like you, y'know, England'd be a jolly dangerous place to live in! (*With a chuckle.*) What d'ye want to do, turn 'em into gentlemen? What's the idea?

Raucous cat-calls from the garden.

MISS MOFFAT: I am beginning to wonder myself.

THE SQUIRE (*sobering*): Anyway, this buyin' 'em out of the mine is a lot of gammon. I own a half-share in it.

MISS MOFFAT: That explains a good deal.

THE SQUIRE: Why don't you take up croquet? Keep your pecker up!

MISS RONBERRY *comes out of the bedroom. She has put on a new dress, and is much prinked up.*

Well, dear lady, anything I can do to make your stay here a happier one——

MISS MOFFAT: Thank you.

THE SQUIRE: I must be getting back. If I know Sir Herbert my best old port will be no more——

MISS MOFFAT (*rising suddenly, and facing him*): Wait a minute.

MISS RONBERRY *pauses on the stairs, and looks inquiringly, from one to the other.*

THE SQUIRE: Yes?

MISS MOFFAT: I know I shall be sticking a pin into a whale, but here are just two words about yourself. You are the Squire Bountiful, are you? Adored by his contented subjects, intelligent and benignly understanding, are you? I should just like to point out that there is a considerable amount of dirt, ignorance, misery and discontent abroad in this world, and that a good deal of it is due to people like you, because you are a stupid, conceited, greedy good-for-nothing, addle-headed nincompoop, and you can go to blue blazes. Good night!

She turns away. A frozen pause. The SQUIRE walks to the front door, and turns.

THE SQUIRE (*majestically*): I perceive that you have been drinking.

He goes.

MISS MOFFAT: That was undignified, but I feel better for it.
She sits on the bench, intensely depressed.

MISS RONBERRY: I am glad, because it *was* plain-spoken, wasn't it? (*Coming down.*) Has he been nasty? So unlike the Squire——

MISS MOFFAT: He was kindness itself. He advised me to go and live in a hole in the ground with my knitting. He has persuaded the owner not to sell.

MISS RONBERRY: Oh dear . . . Of course . . . (*Sitting beside her on the bench, after giving it a cautious flick with her handkerchief*) . . . I always think men know best, don't you?

MISS MOFFAT: Yes.

MISS RONBERRY: I'm wearing my mousseline de soie, and he never even noticed . . . What will you do?

MISS MOFFAT (*rising, her back to the audience*): Sell the house; take this brain-child of a ridiculous spinster, and smother it. Have you got a handkerchief?

MISS RONBERRY: Yes, Miss Moffat. Why?

MISS MOFFAT: I want to blow my nose.

She holds her hand out; MISS RONBERRY *hands her the handkerchief. She blows her nose, and hands the handkerchief back.*

MISS RONBERRY: You ought to have had a cry. (*As* MISS MOFFAT *crosses to the study.*) I love a cry when I'm depressed. Such an advantage over the gentlemen, I always think——

MISS MOFFAT (*opening the study door*): Mr. Jones, will you write letters to the tradespeople and the mine? We are giving up the school . . . (*Coming back to her desk and picking up the waste-paper-basket.*) I suppose we'd better start putting some order into this chaos, and get the business over . . . (*Sitting on the sofa, the basket beside her, picking up five grubby books lying open, one on top of the other.*) What are these filthy exercise books doing among my papers? . . .

MISS RONBERRY (*going to the desk and tidying papers*): Those hooligans just now. They said Mr. Jones had picked them out because they could write English, and would I mind my own some-dreadful-word business.

She crosses and drops some papers in the basket.

MISS MOFFAT (*glancing at the top book*): I set them an essay on

"How I would spend my holiday." (*Throwing it into the basket.*) I must have been mad . . .

> MISS RONBERRY *takes another of the exercise books from her and looks at it as she crosses back to the desk.*

MISS RONBERRY (*reading, laboriously*): "If—I has ever holiday— I has breakfast and talks then dinner and a rest, tea then nothing —then supper then I talk and I go sleep."

MISS MOFFAT: From exhaustion, I suppose.

> BESSIE *comes in from the kitchen, advances to the sofa and takes up her hat.*

(*Tearing up pages.*) Where are you going?

BESSIE: Just another walk, Miss Moffat.

MISS RONBERRY (*as* BESSIE *trails up to the front door, wiping an eye, ostentatiously*): What's the matter, little dear?

BESSIE: Mum's hit me.

MISS RONBERRY: Oh, naughty mum. Why?

BESSIE: 'Cause I told her she was common.

> *She goes.*

MISS RONBERRY (*crossing to the table, and taking up papers*): That child *is* unhappy.

MISS MOFFAT: I can't be bothered with her. (*Glancing at another book.*) Another time I'd have been faintly amused by this one's idea of a holiday, judging by a rather crude drawing.

MISS RONBERRY: What is it?

MISS MOFFAT: A bicycling tour with me in bloomers.

MISS RONBERRY: Tch, tch . . .

> *She crosses to the settle, where she collects more papers.*

MISS MOFFAT (*reading from a third exercise-book*): " 'Holiday-time.' That carefree magic word! What shall it be this year, tobogganing among the eternal snows or tasting the joys of Father Neptune?"

MISS RONBERRY: But that's beautiful! Extraordinary!

MISS MOFFAT: I might think so too if I hadn't seen it in a book open on that desk.

> *She tears up the book and throws it away.*

MISS RONBERRY: Oh!

MISS MOFFAT: No, your Squire was right . . . (*Her eye resting casually and despondently on the last book.*) I have been a stupid and impractical ass, and I can't imagine how——

    A pause. Her eye has caught something on the paper. She begins to read, slowly, with difficulty.

"The mine is dark . . . If a light come in the mine . . . the rivers in the mine will run fast with the voice of many women; the walls will fall in, and it will be the end of the world."

    MISS RONBERRY *is listening, inquiringly.* MORGAN *enters brusquely from the front door. He has made no attempt to wash, but now that he is alone he half-emerges as a truculent arresting boy, with, latent in him, a very strong personality which his immaturity and natural inclination make him shy to display.*

MORGAN: Please, miss, I help with the bell——

MISS RONBERRY: Shhh—the garden—— (*To* MISS MOFFAT.) Do go on——

    MORGAN *moves sulkily towards the garden door.* MISS MOFFAT, *who has not looked up from the paper, begins to read again.*

MISS MOFFAT (*reading*): ". . . So the mine is dark . . ."

    MORGAN *stops, turns, sees what she is holding, and stops abruptly. She continues without having noticed him.*

(*Reading.*) ". . . But when I walk through the Tan—something —shaft, in the dark, I can touch with my hands the leaves on the trees, and underneath . . . (*turning over a page*) . . . where the corn is green."

    A pause.

MORGAN: Go on readin'.

    MISS MOFFAT *looks up at him, then back at the paper.*

MISS MOFFAT (*reading*): ". . . There is a wind in the shaft, not carbon monoxide they talk about, it smell like the sea, only like as if the sea had fresh flowers lying about . . . and that is my holiday."

    A pause. She looks at the front of the book.

Are you Morgan Evans?

MORGAN: Yes, Miss.

MISS MOFFAT: Did you write this?

MORGAN (*after hesitation, sullenly*): No, Miss.

MISS MOFFAT: But it's in your book.

MORGAN: Yes, Miss.

MISS MOFFAT: Then who wrote it?

MORGAN: I dunno, Miss.

    MISS MOFFAT *nods to* MISS RONBERRY, *who patters discreetly into the study.* MORGAN *makes for the garden.*

MISS MOFFAT: Did you write this?

    It is difficult to tell from the crisp severity of her manner that she is expressing a growing inward excitement. MORGAN *stops and looks at her, distrustfully.*

MORGAN: I dunno, Miss . . . (*After hesitating, bursting out*). What iss the matter with it?

MISS MOFFAT: Sit down.

    He stares at her, looks uncertainly towards the garden door, and moves towards the bench.

And take your cap off.

    He stares at her again, on the brink of revolt, then doffs his cap and sits on the bench.

Spelling's deplorable, of course. "Mine" with two "n's", and "leaves" l, e, f, s.

MORGAN (*interested, against his will*): What wass it by rights?

MISS MOFFAT: A "v", to start with.

MORGAN: I never 'eard o' no "v's", Miss.

MOFFAT: Don't call me Miss.

MORGAN: Are you not a Miss?

MISS MOFFAT: Yes I am, but it is not polite.

MORGAN (*uninterested*): Oh.

MISS MOFFAT: You say "Yes, Miss Moffat", or "No, Miss Moffat". M, o, double f, a, t.

MORGAN (*after a pause*): No "v's"?

MISS MOFFAT: No "v's". Where do you live?

MORGAN: Under the ground, Miss.

MISS MOFFAT: I mean your home.

MORGAN: Llyn-y-Mwyn, Miss . . . Moffat. Four miles from 'ere.

MISS MOFFAT: How big is it?

MORGAN: Four 'ouses and a beer-'ouse.

MISS MOFFAT: Have you any hobbies?

MORGAN: Oh yes.

MISS MOFFAT: What?

MORGAN: Rum.

MISS MOFFAT: Rum?

He takes his bottle from his pocket, holds it up, and puts it back.

Do you live with your parents?

MORGAN: No, by me own self. Me mother iss dead, and me father and me four big brothers wass in the Big Shaft Accident when I wass ten.

MISS MOFFAT: Killed?

MORGAN: Oh yes, everybody wass.

MISS MOFFAT: What sort of man was your father?

MORGAN: 'E was a mongrel.

MISS MOFFAT: A what?

MORGAN: 'E had a dash of English. He learned it to me.

MISS MOFFAT: D'you go to chapel?

MORGAN: No thank you.

MISS MOFFAT: Who taught you to read and write?

MORGAN: Tott?

MISS MOFFAT: Taught. The verb "to teach".

MORGAN: Oh, teached.

MISS MOFFAT: Who taught you?

MORGAN: I did.

MISS MOFFAT: Why?

MORGAN: I dunno.

MISS MOFFAT: What books have you read?

MORGAN: Books? A bit of the Bible and a book that a feller from the Plas kitchen nab for me.

MISS MOFFAT: What was it?

MORGAN: *The Ladies' Companion.*

A pause. She rises, and walks thoughtfully up towards her desk, studying him. He sits uncomfortably, twirling his cap between grimy fingers.

(*Rising, at last, making to don his cap.*) Can I go now, pliss——

MISS MOFFAT (*suddenly, decisively*): No.

He sits, taken aback. She walks round the bench and stands near the garden door, facing him.

MISS MOFFAT: Do you want to learn any more?

MORGAN: No thank you.

MISS MOFFAT: Why not?

MORGAN: The other men would have a good laugh.

MISS MOFFAT: I see.

A pause. She crosses slowly to the sofa, turns, and faces him again.

Have you ever written anything before this exercise?

MORGAN: No.

MISS MOFFAT: Why not?

MORGAN: Nobody never ask me to. (*After a pause, truculently, feeling her eyes on him.*) What iss the matter with it?

MISS MOFFAT (*sitting, looking thoughtfully at the book*): Nothing's the matter with it. Whether it means anything is too early for me to say, but it shows exceptional talent for a boy in your circumstances.

MORGAN (*after blinking and hesitating*): Terrible long words, Miss Moffat.

MISS MOFFAT: This shows that you are very clever.

A pause. He looks up slowly, not sure if he has heard aright, looks at her searchingly, then away again. His mind is working, uncertainly, but swiftly.

MORGAN: Oh.

MISS MOFFAT: Have you ever been told that before?

MORGAN: It iss news to me.

MISS MOFFAT: What effect does the news have on you?

MORGAN: It iss a bit sudden. (*After a pause.*) It makes me that I——(*Hesitating, then plunging.*)—I want to get more clever still. (*Looking slowly, wonderingly round the room.*) I want to know what iss—behind of all them books. . . .

MISS MOFFAT (*after studying him a moment, calling suddenly*): Miss Ronberry! . . . (*To him.*) Can you come to-morrow?

MORGAN (*taken by surprise*): To-morrow—no—I am workin' on the six till four shift——

MISS MOFFAT: Then can you be here at five?

MORGAN: Five—no, not before seven, Miss—six miles to walk——

MISS MOFFAT: Oh yes, of course—seven then. In the meantime I'll correct this for spelling and grammar.

MORGAN (*staring at her, fascinated, after a pause*): Yes, Miss Moffat.
She walks briskly towards the study. He has not moved. She turns and looks at him.

MISS MOFFAT: That will be all. Good night.

MORGAN (*after a pause*): Good night, Miss Moffat.
He goes towards the front door, putting on his cap.

MISS MOFFAT: Are you the one I spanked?
He turns at the door, looks at her, blinks, and goes.
(*Calling, excitedly.*) Miss Ronberry! Mr. Jones!
MISS RONBERRY runs in from the study.

MISS RONBERRY: Yes?

MISS MOFFAT: I have been a deuce of a fool. It doesn't matter about the barn; we are going to start the school, in a small way at first, in this room. . . . And I am going to get those youngsters out of that mine if I have to black my face and go down and fetch them myself! Get Jonesy before he posts those letters, and tell those others I'll be ready for them in five minutes. We are going on with the school!

MISS RONBERRY, who has punctuated this speech with a series of nods, scampers into the study, rather dazed. Her voice is heard, calling: "We are going on with the school!"
The door shuts behind her.
MISS MOFFAT looks down at the exercise-book she is still carrying.

MISS MOFFAT (*reading*): ". . . and when I walk—in the dark . . . I can touch with my hands . . . where the corn is green . . ."
The fitful joyous clang of the school bell above.
She looks up, excited, listening.

CURTAIN

ACT II

SCENE I

An early evening in August, two years later; the sun is still bright.

The room is now a complete jumble of living-room and school-room, and there is every sign of cheerful overcrowding. The table in the window recess is replaced by two school-desks; the table and its small chair are pushed behind the sofa; the spinning-wheel has been removed; a school-desk stands isolated between the big open-top desk and the sofa; between the sofa and the bay window, two rows of four school-desks each, squeezed together and facing the audience at an angle. Charts, maps, an alphabet list and a slate with writing on it, are pinned up higgledy-piggledy over all the books; a large world globe on the shelf; hat-pegs have been fixed irregularly on the stair-banisters. Books overflow everywhere, all over the dresser especially, in place of plates; the hat-pegs are loaded with caps and hats; MISS MOFFAT's hat is still perched on the knob at the foot of the stairs; her cloak hangs on a hook on the back of the front door; an easel and blackboard lie against the sofa, with "Constantinople is the capital of Turkey" written across in MISS RONBERRY's tremulous handwriting; stuffed fish in a glass case on top of a book-case. The lamp on the table has been removed. Potted plants on the window-sills.

Before the curtain rises, voices are heard singing, in harmony, in Welsh, "Bugeilio'r Gwenyth Gwyn": children shrill, sweet and self-confident, reinforced by harmony from older boys and parents, especially SARAH.

The room seems full of people; MISS RONBERRY *stands perched on the tiny stool between the sofa and the foot of the stairs, her back to the audience, conducting stiffly with a ruler;* MR. JONES *is crouched in the desk-chair, correcting exercises at the open desk.* SARAH, *two older peasant women in shawls, and three older men in their shabby best stand crowded behind the eight desks and in the window recess. In the front row of desks sit* ROBBART, IDWAL, *a little girl, and* GLYN THOMAS; *in the second sit another little boy, another little girl,* BESSIE, *and* WILL HUGHES. *In another desk pushed provisionally next the front row sits* JOHN OWEN, *and in the other isolated one sits* OLD TOM, *an elderly, distinguished-looking, grey-bearded peasant, his cap and stick before him, carried away by the music.*

BESSIE *is silent, bored, and prettier than ever, though still dressed as a sober little schoolgirl. The boys we saw before as miners are clean and almost spruce; the parents follow every movement of* MISS RONBERRY'S *with avid curiosity. The pupils have slates and slate-pencils in front of them.*

The song is sung through to the end.

MISS RONBERRY: Now that was quite better. Full of splendid feeling, and nice and precise as well. Have you all got my English translation?

THE PUPILS: Yes, Miss Ronberry.

MISS RONBERRY: Are you all quite sure of the meaning of "Thou lovedest him, fair maid, that doth not love thee back"?

THE PUPILS (*as she climbs down from her stool*): Yes, Miss Ronberry.

OLD TOM (*singing stentoriously, in broken English*): . . . "That doth not luff thee . . . ba-a-ck!"

MISS RONBERRY: Capital, Mr. Tom.

She takes a small handbell from a hook beneath the stairs, rings it vigorously, and hangs it up again; nobody moves.

Home sweet home, children! . . . (*Gaily, as they all study her like owls.*) Boys and girls, come out to play!

IDWAL: Please, Miss Ronberry, can we have some more?

MISS RONBERRY: Well, just the tiniest lesson. (*Climbing on to her stool again.*) We must keep to the curriculum. Now what would you like?

IDWAL: Please, Miss Ronberry, how do you spell it?

MISS RONBERRY: What, dear?

OLD TOM: Curriculum!

MISS RONBERRY: What would you like? The rivers of Europe or King Alfred and the cakes?

36

OLD TOM (*ecstatically*): Multiplication table!

MISS RONBERRY: Twice six are twelve!

THE PUPILS: Twice seven are fourteen—twice eight are sixteen——

> *They continue up to "Twice twelve are twenty-four", and stop.*

OLD TOM: Twice thirteen are twenty-six!

MISS RONBERRY: Capital—school dismiss!

> *The children and grown-ups bustle and chatter. One or two scribble on their slates; another rubs out what he has written; others run over for hats and coats.*

IDWAL (*after looking out of the open garden door, calling to the others*): Dyma'r fistress!

> *The whole room, except BESSIE, who remains seated, stand silent and respectful while MISS MOFFAT walks in from the garden. She is more alert and business-like than ever, carries a tiny portable desk under one arm, and is studying an exercise book. She nods pleasantly to the room, goes upstairs and into her bedroom; as she sets foot on the stairs the hubbub starts again abruptly, and the crowd saunter or hurry chattily through the front door; during this ROBBART takes the blackboard and easel, leans them against the settle and puts away the stool, while JOHN OWEN shuts the garden door and pushes his desk into the corner near the grandfather's clock. The crowd finally trickle out, shepherded by MISS RONBERRY, who shuts the door after them. Besides BESSIE, there are left OLD TOM, standing immovable next to his desk, studying MISS RONBERRY as if she were a book, and IDWAL, who hovers eagerly on the other side.*
>
> *The overlapping crowd dialogue in this scene could be allotted roughly from the following:*

1. Be'di'r gloch, Merry?
   Chwarter i bump.

2. What iss the next thing in the multiplication?
   Wn i ddim yn wyr—gofyn iddi——

3. Why issn't there any geography now?
   Friday geography, Thursday to-day——
   Pnawn dydd iau, te, hanner awr wedi tri——

4. Mi ddylaswn fod yn pobi heddyw——
A dwidi gadal y cig yn y popdy——
Mi fydd eich cegin chi ar dan, Mrs. Pugh——

5. IDWAL: 'Nhad, gai fynd i chwara yn nghae John Davies——
OLDER MAN (*answering him*): Ddim heddyw—dwisho ti
gartre——

6. Yfory d'wi am drio sgwennu llythyr——
Os gynnachi steel-pen golew?
Mae'na gymaint o flots!
Dwi wedi sgwennu llythyr at fy nain, wni ddim be ddidi'thi
. . . Welsochi 'rioed eiriau fel ene?

7. Fedri'thi ddim canu fel Cymraes, digon siwr——
Mae'r hen ddyn am ofyn rwbeth iddi eto—drychwch arno——
Mi gollith'o ei Gymraeg cyn bo hir——

8. Idwal, what you looking so sorry—always wanting to know
something——

9. Mae genni just ddigon o amser i gyrraedd at y llyn——
Mae'r dwr yn rhy oer i ymdrochi——
Nag ydi—mae'r haul wedi bod yn rhy boeth heddyw——

10. Neidi ofyn i Morgan ddwad——
Feder o ddim——
Mae o'n gweithio'n rhy galed——

MISS RONBERRY *shuts the door on the crowd, with a sigh of
relief, and finds herself between* OLD TOM *and* IDWAL.
IDWAL: Miss Ronberry, please, what is four times fourteen?
MISS RONBERRY: Thank you so much for the flowers, Idwal,
dear.
IDWAL: Yes, Miss Ronberry.
He follows the others, calling after them by name.
MISS RONBERRY (*nervously*): Is there anything *you* would like
to know, Mr. Tom?

OLD TOM: Where iss Shakespeare?

MISS RONBERRY: Where? . . . Shakespeare, Mr. Tom, was a very great writer.

OLD TOM: Writer? Like the Beibl?

MISS RONBERRY: Like the Bible.

OLD TOM (*looking at her doubtfully*): Dear me, and me thinkin' the man was a place. (*Following the others, muttering sadly.*) If I iss been born fifty years later, I iss been top of the class. . . .

MISS RONBERRY (*shutting the front door after him*): Oh dear . . . (*Tidying the desks.*) Miss Moffat has been doing grammar with Form Two under the pear-tree for an hour, she must be dead . . . (*To* BESSIE, *who is climbing over the desks.*) Why did you not get up when she crossed?

BESSIE: My foot went to sleep.

Her manner is more impudent than when we last saw her.

MISS RONBERRY (*coming down to the sofa*): That, dear, is a naughty fib.

BESSIE (*subsiding into* OLD TOM'S *desk*): If you want to know, Miss Ronberry, I feel quite faint sometimes, as if my heart'd stopped and the world was coming to an end.

MISS MOFFAT *comes downstairs, still carrying her portable desk, and studying her exercise-book.*

MISS RONBERRY (*with guileless solicitude*): Bessie dear, how horrid!

MR. JONES: It may be in the nature of a premonition.

MISS RONBERRY: A what?

She perches on the edge of a desk in the recess and tries to get ink off her knuckles with pumice-stone. MISS MOFFAT *lays her portable desk on the table, and paces slowly towards the front door, studying her exercise-book.*

MR. JONES: I had a premonition once. Like a wave of the ocean breakin' on a sea-shell. Something had said to me that morning: "Walk, and think, and keep off the food, for thirteen hours." So I ordered my supper, and I went. Towards the end of the day, I was sittin' on a stile in a cloak of meditation; and a voice roared at me: "John Goronwy Jones, to-morrow morning is the end of the world!"

MISS MOFFAT: And was it?

MR. JONES (*sadly*): It was eight years ago. It was a splendid experience.

He goes back to his correcting.

MISS MOFFAT: Which proves how much the gift of prophecy can owe to an empty stomach. . . . Anybody seen a Greek book? (*Picking up a tiny volume from under a pile of papers on the desk.*) Here it is . . .

MISS RONBERRY: Greek, Miss Moffat?

MISS MOFFAT: Morgan Evans is starting Greek this month.

MISS RONBERRY: No! I didn't know you knew Greek?

MISS MOFFAT (*hurrying upstairs*): I don't; I've just got to keep one day ahead of him and trust to luck.

She disappears into her bedroom.

MISS RONBERRY: To think that two years ago he hardly knew English!

BESSIE: Stuck-up teacher's pet.

MISS RONBERRY: You must not think that, dear, Miss Moffat says he is clever.

BESSIE: He always looks right through me, so I don't know, I'm sure. Stuck-up teacher's pet. . . . I got some scent on my hands, Mr. Jones, like to smell them?

MR. JONES (*timidly*): No, thank you, Bessie, I can smell them from here, thank you.

BESSIE (*sniffing her hands, softly*): Ooh, it's lovely . . .

MISS RONBERRY: She has some wonderful plans for him—I can tell by her manner. *I* think she is trying to send him to one of those Church schools to be a curate. Would not that be exciting?

BESSIE (*resting her head on her hands, indolently*): I think she's ridin' for a fall.

MISS RONBERRY: Bessie! Why?

BESSIE: All this orderin' 'im about. I've got eyes in my head, if she hasn't, and he's gettin' sick of it. *I* think a lady ought to be dainty. She's no idea.

    MISS MOFFAT *appears at the top of the stairs, wiping her hands with a towel.*

MISS MOFFAT: Evans!

A pause. MORGAN *comes in from the study. He is now seventeen. He is dressed in a shabby country suit, and is at the moment the submissive schoolboy, very different from the first act. He carries a sheet of writing and a pen.* MISS MOFFAT'S *attitude to him seems purely impersonal. The others watch them.*

MISS MOFFAT: Finished?

MORGAN: Yes, Miss Moffat.

MISS MOFFAT: How many pages?

MORGAN: Nine.

MISS MOFFAT: Three too many. Boil down to six. Have you got those lines of Voltaire?

MORGAN (*showing the paper*): Yes, Miss Moffat.

MISS MOFFAT: It's just five—have your walk now, good and brisk . . . (*taking his cap from a peg and tossing it to him*) . . . here.

MORGAN (*starting for the front door, putting his pen behind his ear*): Yes, Miss Moffat.

MISS MOFFAT: But kill two birds and get the Voltaire by heart. If you can ever argue a point like that, you'll do. Back in twenty minutes—and take your pen from behind your ear.

She disappears into her bedroom. Her manner is too matter of fact to be unkind, but MORGAN *is not taking it well; he throws his pen on to* BESSIE'S *desk; he has stopped close to her, and catches her eye.*

BESSIE: Now turn a somersault and beg.

He looks at her with contempt. She returns his stare brazenly; he is unwillingly attracted by her. She turns to see if the others are noticing. MISS RONBERRY *is busy with her pumice-stone in the window recess and* MR. JONES *is engrossed in his work.* BESSIE *looks away from them all, suddenly soft and mysterious.*

BESSIE: Can you smell scent?

MORGAN (*after a pause*): Yes.

BESSIE (*dreamily*): Nice, isn't it?

MORGAN: I don't know, I never come across scent before. (*Correcting himself unwillingly.*) I did never come across . . . scent before . . .

BESSIE: Bright, aren't you? Don't you ever get tired of lessons?

She begins to sing, softly, at him. He goes to the front door, turns, arrested by her singing, then goes, banging the door. She flings down her slate with annoyance.

BESSIE (*darkly*): There we go. And my mummy ought to be back soon, and then we'll know somethin'.

MR. JONES: What is the matter? Where has she gone?

BESSIE: One of her prayer meetings. Twenty miles to shake a tambourine in the open air, I think it's wicked. . . . She ought to be just in time, and then we'll know.

MR. JONES: Know what?

BESSIE: About that horrid Morgan Evans. It's been lessons every night with teacher, hasn't it, since we left the mine? And long walks in between, to blow the cobwebs away? But the last week or two we've been breaking our journey, so we've heard.

MR. JONES: How do you mean?

BESSIE (*triumphantly*): A glass of rum next door at the Gwesmor Arms and then another, and then another!

MR. JONES (*perturbed*): Oh. . . . Whoever told you that?

BESSIE: A little bird. (*As he crosses and sits at the table.*) And if my mummy's sciatica's better she's going to jump up and look over the frosty part and then we'll *know*.

MRS. WATTY *hurries in through the front door, in high spirits. She wears an ill-fitting Militant Righteousness Corps uniform, and carries an umbrella and a brown-paper parcel.*

MRS. WATTY: Guess what's 'appened to me!

BESSIE: What?

MRS. WATTY: I'm a Sergeant-Major!

MISS MOFFAT *has come out on to the landing; her hair is down and she is brushing it.*

MISS MOFFAT: Watty, you're not!

MRS. WATTY: Oh, ma'am, I didn't see you——

MISS MOFFAT: Tell me more!

MRS. WATTY: You remember Sergeant-Major 'Opkins desertin' in Cardiff and marryin' a sailor?

MISS MOFFAT: Yes?

MRS. WATTY: Well, last week, not two months after she give up the Corpse, she was dead!

MISS MOFFAT: And you've stepped into her shoes?

MRS. WATTY: They're a bit on the big side; but I can put a bit of paper in. The uniform fits lovely, though. (*Moving towards the kitchen.*) I'll get you a cup o' tea and an egg, ma'am, you never 'ad that cold meat, ma'am, I'll be bound?

MISS MOFFAT: Folk eat too much anyway.

She goes back into her bedroom.

BESSIE: Did you jump?

MRS. WATTY (*coming back into the room*): Just caught 'im. (*To* MR. JONES, *sorrowfully.*) 'Avin' a good swig, sir . . . (*To* BESSIE.) Don't you dare tell 'er, you little dollymop, or I'll rattle your bones——

MISS MOFFAT reappears and comes downstairs, finishing doing up her hair, her little book between her teeth.

MISS MOFFAT: Was it a nice service, Watty?

MISS RONBERRY walks round the desks and begins to take an interest.

MRS. WATTY: Beautiful, ma'am. They said they 'oped the late Sergeant-Major was gone where we all want to go, but with 'er having deserted they couldn't be sure. Then we saved three sinners. (*Prodding* MR. JONES *with her umbrella.*) *You* ought to been there. . . . And the collection! (*Going.*) I 'adn't seed so much oof since the Great Liverpool Exhibition.

MISS RONBERRY: But they didn't make a collection at the Liverpool Exhibition, did they?

MRS. WATTY: No, but I did.

She goes into the kitchen. MR. JONES *erects the board on its easel next to the stairs, takes an old duster which is trailing from his pocket, rubs out what is written, takes out a chalk and copies a diagram carefully and indistinguishably on to the board from the paper in his hand.*

MISS MOFFAT wanders towards the front door, studying.

BESSIE: Please, Miss Moffat, can I have the money for my ticket?

MISS MOFFAT: What ticket?

BESSIE: For Tregarna Fair to-morrow. You said I could go.

MISS MOFFAT: On the contrary, I said you couldn't. Not in school hours.

She studies. BESSIE *sighs and tries to look ill.*

MISS RONBERRY: Are you feeling better, dear?

BESSIE: No, Miss Ronberry. It's all this sittin' down. It's been going on for two years now. I heard tell it ends in everythin' rottin' away.

MISS MOFFAT (*looking up*): What's rotting away?

MISS RONBERRY: Bessie says she's been sitting down for two years.

MISS MOFFAT: She's lucky. My feet feel as if I've been standing for the same length of time. (*Sitting at the open desk and looking at some papers on a book.*) What are these, Ron?

MISS RONBERRY: Two more accounts, I fear.

MISS MOFFAT: Oh yes. The Liddell and Scott and Evans's new suit——(*seeing the amounts*) tch. . . . (*Cheerfully.*) I shall have to sell out a couple more shares, I expect.

MISS RONBERRY: Oh dear.

MISS MOFFAT: Not at all. (*Unlacing her boots.*) It's easy to squander money, and its easy to hoard it; the most difficult thing in the world is to use it. And if I've learnt to use it, I've *done* something. That's better . . . (*Rubbing her hands.*) My plans are laid, Ron my dear, my plans are laid! But don't ask me what I'm hatching, because I can't tell you till to-morrow.

MISS RONBERRY: You are wonderful!

MISS MOFFAT: Go to Halifax. I'm enjoying myself.

MISS RONBERRY *crosses, sits on the sofa, and peers at her papers.* MISS MOFFAT *puts her head in her hands and studies her Greek dictionary.* BESSIE *sighs again, ostentatiously.* MISS MOFFAT *looks at her.*

MISS MOFFAT: Bessie Watty, what is all this dying duck business?

BESSIE: Yes, Miss Moffat.

MISS MOFFAT: Don't "yes, Miss Moffat" me. Explain yourself.

The instinctive hostility between them is strong.

BESSIE: My mummy said all these lessons is bad for my inside.

MISS MOFFAT (*turning back to her book*): She told me they stop you eating sweets, but perhaps *I* am telling the lies.

BESSIE: Yes, Miss Moffat.

MISS MOFFAT: What's the matter with your inside?

BESSIE: It goes round and round through sittin' down. P'raps what I want is a change.

MISS MOFFAT: What you want is castor oil. (*Muttering.*) "Adelphos, a brother" . . . There is nothing to prevent you going for walks between lessons. You can go for one now, as far as Sarah Pugh Postman, to see if my new chalks have arrived. (*Looking round at* BESSIE, *as the latter stares before her without moving, her inward rage mounting.*) Quick march.

> *She goes back to her book.* BESSIE *rises, moves sulkily towards the front door, stops, and turns. The only sound is the scratch of* MR. JONES'S *chalk on the blackboard.*

BESSIE: I'm not goin'.

> *The other three turn and look at her, astounded.*

MISS MOFFAT: What did you say?

BESSIE: I'm not goin'. Everybody's against me . . . I'm goin' to throw myself off a cliff, an' kill myself. . . . It'll make a nice case in the papers, me in pieces at the bottom of a cliff! . . . I'm goin' mad, mad, and I'm goin' to kill myself, nothin's goin' to stop me—stone dead at the bottom of a cliff—ah—ah—ah——

> *She has gradually warmed up into a fit of hysteria, half natural half induced; her paroxysm rises to a crescendo of screaming and wringing of hands; spoilt, unfortunately, by* MRS. WATTY *striding in from the kitchen with a cupful of cold water which she throws into her daughter's face.* BESSIE *splutters, chokes, and subsides into inarticulate moans of self-pity.*

MRS. WATTY (*to* MISS MOFFAT): I made a mess o' your rug, ma'am, but it's worth it. She's got bad blood, this girl, mark my word.

MISS RONBERRY: She'll catch her death!

MRS. WATTY: Nothing like cold water, ma'am. I learnt that with her father. 'E was foreign, you know.

> *She goes back into the kitchen.* BESSIE *stands sniffing and gulping.* MISS MOFFAT *studies her with distaste.*

MISS MOFFAT: And how do you feel after that?

BESSIE: I can't remember anything. I'm in a comma.

MISS MOFFAT (*taking her by the arm and pushing her upstairs*):

We'll sit on our bed for an hour with the door locked, shall we, and *try* to remember? And next week you go away into service—and see how we like that——

> *She pushes her out of sight into the passage; a door bangs; the noise of a lock turning.*
>
> MISS MOFFAT *comes downstairs, tucking the key into her petticoat pocket.* MR. JONES *turns the blackboard round back to front on its easel.*

I must count her as one of my failures. Fish out of water, of course. Guttersnipe species—if there is such a fish. She'll be more at home in service . . . (*Muttering.*) "Dendron, a tree——"

MISS RONBERRY: I beg your pardon? . . . Oh, Miss Moffat, I am bursting with curiosity—your plans for Morgan Evans . . . is it a curateship?

MISS MOFFAT (*slowly, amused*): No, it isn't a curateship.

> *She laughs happily, walks towards the desk, and takes up an exercise-book.*

MISS RONBERRY: I really don't see anything funny about curates. (*To* MR. JONES.) I mean, there is nothing *wrong* with curates, is there?

MR. JONES: No, except that they ought to go to chapel.

MISS MOFFAT: Who has been writing in here?

> MRS. WATTY *appears at the kitchen door.*

MRS. WATTY: Your egg, ma'am!

MISS MOFFAT: "Bessie Watty has the face of an angel"!

MISS RONBERRY: What an extraordinary——

MISS MOFFAT: But I know the writing——

> *She looks again;* MR. JONES *blinks behind his spectacles, takes his hat from a peg, and makes to pass her.*

MISS MOFFAT: John Goronwy Jones, I'm ashamed of you.

MR. JONES: I shall see you to-morrow if we are spared.

MISS RONBERRY (*shocked*): Oh!

MR. JONES: You all misjudge that little girl. She has the face of a good woman in the melting-pot.

MISS MOFFAT: I've got the face of a good woman too, and well out of the melting-pot, but I don't think I'd ever find it in writing.

She goes into the kitchen, chuckling, as MISS RONBERRY *puts on her hat in a little mirror in front of the study door.*

MRS. WATTY: I never thought I'd live to call *you* a dirty old man.

She follows MISS MOFFAT *into the kitchen.* MR. JONES *goes out through the front door.* MISS RONBERRY *sighs a little disconsolately into the mirror, tries to look like an angel, fails, and sighs again. The front door opens abruptly and* MORGAN *appears. He is dishevelled, and it is fairly apparent that he has been drinking. His manner is defiant, and he does not remove his cap. The door bangs behind him.*

MISS RONBERRY: Oh, it's you, Morgan . . . (*Back at the mirror.*) Miss Moffat is having something to eat.

MORGAN: And I have been having something to drink, so we are quits.

MISS RONBERRY (*looking round at him, sharply, the unpleasant truth dawning on her*): I will tell her that you are back——

MORGAN (*looking away, breathing hard*): I don't want to see no Miss Moffat.

MISS RONBERRY (*bravely*): You mean "I don't want to see Miss Moffat." The double negative——

MORGAN: Now don't you start! . . . (*Bearing down on her.*) I like the double negative, it says what I want the way I like, and I am *not* goin' to stand *no* interferences from *no*body! (*Taking his paper from his pocket and kicking it savagely into a corner of the room.*) Voltaire indeed . . .

MISS RONBERRY: Morgan! I've never seen you like this before!

MORGAN: You haven't, have you? (*In a rising torrent of invective, getting more Welsh as it goes on.*) Well, now I come to think of it, I haven't neither, not for two years, and I'm surprised by meself, and shocked by meself! Goin' inside one o' them public houses and puttin' me nice clean boots on that dirty rail, and me dainty lady-fingers on that detestable mucky counter! Pourin' poison rum down me nice clean teeth, and spittin' in a spittoon—what's come over you, Morgan Evans? You come back to your little cage, and if you comb hair and wash hands and get your grammar right and forget you was once the Middle-weight Champion of the

Glasynglo Miners, we might give you a nice bit of sewin' to do
. . . (*Turning back to the front door, muttering.*) Where's that Bessie
Watty, sendin' her mother to spy on me, I'll knock her bloody
block off . . .

MISS RONBERRY (*outraged*): Morgan Evans, *language!* Don't
you dare use an expression like that to me again!

MORGAN (*turning back on her*): I got plenty of others, thank you,
and they are all comin' out. I am goin' to surprise quite a few——

 He stops short and pulls off his cap as MISS MOFFAT *enters
 from the kitchen.*

MISS MOFFAT (*pouring milk into a cup from a jug*): Have a good
walk, Evans?

MORGAN (*controlling himself, avoiding* MISS RONBERRY'S *eye*): Yes,
Miss Moffat.

MISS MOFFAT (*sitting on the sofa, drinking*): Can you repeat the
Voltaire?

MORGAN: Not yet.

MISS MOFFAT: It's very short.

MORGAN: Paper blowed away.

MISS MOFFAT: Oh. Copy it again, will you, and bring it to me.

MORGAN (*muttering*): Yes, Miss Moffat.

 He goes towards the study.

MISS MOFFAT (*holding out the jug*): Would you like a drink?

 He starts, looks round at her and sees the milk.

MORGAN: No thank you.

 He goes into the study. MISS MOFFAT *takes her little book
 again from her pocket and opens it.*

MISS MOFFAT: I hope he's not going to be slow at French.
It'll make the Greek so much more difficult——

MISS RONBERRY (*timidly*): You don't think perhaps all this—
in his situation—is rather sudden for him? I mean——

MISS MOFFAT: Not for him, my dear. He has the most
brilliantly receptive brain I've ever come across. Don't tell him
so, but he has.

MISS RONBERRY: I know his *brain* is all right——

MISS MOFFAT (*absently*): I'm very pleased with his progress,
on the whole . . .

A knock at the front door. MISS RONBERRY *looks at her uncertainly, then moves towards the door.* MISS MOFFAT *suddenly remembers something, and stops her.*

Wait a minute! (*Rising, hurrying to the bay window, and peering out towards the front door, and hurrying down again urgently.*) Yes, it is . . .

MISS RONBERRY: Who?

MISS MOFFAT (*sitting on the sofa and doing up her boots, hastily*): Royalty, the Conservatives and all the Grand Lamas rolled into one. The Squire.

MISS RONBERRY: The Squire! (*In a panic.*) Oh, *my!*

MISS MOFFAT (*lacing*): It is indeed, oh my——

MISS RONBERRY: But he hasn't been here since that dreadful evening——

MISS MOFFAT: I behaved more stupidly that night than I ever have in my life, and that's saying something——

MISS RONBERRY: But why is he here now?

MISS MOFFAT (*placing the milk-jug and cup on the table*): Never you mind. . . . All I can tell you is that it is to do with Morgan Evans, and that it is vital I make the right impression——

MISS RONBERRY (*as* MISS MOFFAT *runs upstairs*): What sort of impression?

MISS MOFFAT: Helpless and clinging, or as near as dammit——
    She disappears into her room, as there is a second impatient knock at the front door.

MISS RONBERRY (*timidly*): Come in!
    The door opens and the GROOM *appears.*

THE GROOM (*announcing*): The Squire.
    The SQUIRE *follows the* GROOM, *who retires and shuts the door.*

THE SQUIRE: Good afternoon.
    His manner is stiff and careful. He is dressed in a summer lounge suit, and holds his hat in his hand. He looks round the room with cold disapproval.

MISS RONBERRY: Your hat, Squire——

THE SQUIRE: No, thank you, I am not staying.

MISS RONBERRY: Oh dear, I do look a sketch . . .

THE SQUIRE: So this is the seat of learning.

MISS RONBERRY: We are always on the point of a good spring-

49

clean. How dreadful that we have no refreshment to offer you!

THE SQUIRE: Has she given it up, then? . . . You can tell her from me that I am not here to be insulted again.

MISS RONBERRY: Oh, I'm sure you aren't! I mean——

THE SQUIRE: (*ruminantly*): She called me an addle-headed nincompoop.

> MISS MOFFAT *comes downstairs, a lace shawl draped over her shoulders. She carries a bowl of flowers.*

MISS MOFFAT: Miss Ronberry, dear, my roses are dying—would you pour out a little water for them, I have such a headache I don't think—— (*Feigning surprise.*) *Squire!*

THE SQUIRE (*as she crosses to him, hand outraised*): You wrote to me Perhaps you have forgotten.

MISS MOFFAT: How could I forget! I only thought that after the overwrought fashion of my behaviour at our last meeting you must ignore my very nervous invitation—— Miss Ronberry, a chair, dear, for the Squire——

> *Startled,* MISS RONBERRY *looks for a chair, then back at her. Puzzled, and trying not to unbend, the* SQUIRE *stands examining* MISS MOFFAT.

THE SQUIRE: I have not a great deal of time to spare, I fear.

MISS MOFFAT (*sitting on the lower end of the sofa*): Of course you haven't, I was just saying to Miss Ronberry, he's so busy he'll *never* be able to fit it in! Miss Ronberry dear, would you get some water for them?

> *She hands the bowl to* MISS RONBERRY, *who passes the* SQUIRE *and goes into the garden, bewildered.*

Tell me, Squire, how did your prize-giving fare this afternoon?

THE SQUIRE: Rather a bore, y'know.

MISS MOFFAT: I had so hoped to see you judge. I love flowers.

THE SQUIRE: It wasn't flowers. It was cows.

MISS MOFFAT: Oh. It was your speech I wanted to hear, of course; I heard you made such an amusing one at the Croquet.

THE SQUIRE (*breaking into a smile*): Oh, did they tell you about that? Rather a good pun, eh? (*Laughing reminiscently.*) Ha ha . . . I—may sit down?

MISS MOFFAT: Do!

THE SQUIRE (*after looking at* BESSIE's *desk, and finally choosing the top end of the sofa*): I thought Griffiths the butcher was going to laugh his napper off.

MISS MOFFAT: Indeed. . . . Do you know, Squire, that makes me rather proud?

THE SQUIRE (*stiffening again*): Proud? Why?

MISS MOFFAT (*innocently*): Because he would not have understood a word if his little girls hadn't learnt English at my school.

THE SQUIRE: Oh. Never thought of it like that . . . (*As she puts her hand to her head.*) Headache?

MISS MOFFAT: Squire, you see before you a tired woman. We live and learn, and I have learnt how right you were that night. I have worked my fingers to the bone battering my head against a stone wall.

THE SQUIRE (*puzzled*): But I heard you were a spiffing success.

MISS MOFFAT: Oh, no.

THE SQUIRE (*muttering*): It's fair of you to admit it, I must say.

MISS MOFFAT: You see, in one's womanly enthusiasm one forgets that the qualities vital to success in this sort of venture are completely lacking in one: intelligence, courage and authority. . . . the qualities, in short, of a man.

THE SQUIRE: Come, come, you mustn't be too hard on yourself, y'know. After all, you've meant well.

MISS MOFFAT: It's kind of you to say that.

THE SQUIRE: What about this Jones chappie?

MISS MOFFAT: He's a dear creature, but . . . (*soberly*) . . . I have no wish to be fulsome, I mean a man like yourself.

THE SQUIRE: I see.

MISS MOFFAT: One gets into such muddles! You'd never believe!

THE SQUIRE: Well . . . I've never been on your side, but I'm sorry to hear you've come a cropper. When are you giving it up?

MISS MOFFAT (*taken aback*): Oh. . . . That again is difficult; I have all my widow's mite, as it were, in the venture——

A knock at the study door. MORGAN *appears, carrying a paper. He has regained his self-control. He hesitates on seeing there is a visitor, and makes to go back.*

MORGAN: Please excuse me——

MISS MOFFAT (*hastily*): It's all right, Evans. Have you copied it? On my desk, will you?

MORGAN (*bowing, and crossing in front of the sofa*): Excuse me, sir . . . (*Turning back his head.*) Good afternoon, sir.

THE SQUIRE (*eyeing him curiously as he places the paper on the desk*): Good afternoon, my boy.

MORGAN (*bowing, before crossing him again*): Excuse me, sir . . . (*Turning at the study door, and bowing again.*) Thank you.

   He goes.

THE SQUIRE: Nice well-spoken lad. Relative?

MISS MOFFAT: No. A pupil. He used to be one of your miners.

THE SQUIRE: No!

MISS MOFFAT: I'm glad you thought he was a nice well-spoken boy.

THE SQUIRE (*vaguely*): Yes. . . . One of my miners, interesting . . .

MISS MOFFAT: Because he is the problem I should like your advice about.

THE SQUIRE: What's he been up to, poaching?

MISS MOFFAT: No.

THE SQUIRE: A bit o' muslin?

MISS MOFFAT (*amused*): No, no. . . . There are none, anyway——

THE SQUIRE (*suddenly shrewd*): What about the little Cockney filly?

MISS MOFFAT: Bessie Watty? Oh no, I assure you—— (*amused*)—she's a schoolgirl——

THE SQUIRE: I dunno, all these young people growing up together, y'know—eh?

MISS MOFFAT: I think it's good for them. . . . No, there's nothing of that sort—— (*getting back to the point*)—but he's a problem just the same. And like a true woman I have to scream for help to a man. To you.

THE SQUIRE (*after a pause, completely won*): Scream away, dear lady, scream away!

MISS MOFFAT (*earnestly*): Well, he's . . . clever.

THE SQUIRE: Oh, is he? Good at figures, and all that? Because if he is, there's no reason why I shouldn't put him in my Mine Office, as junior office boy. (*Munificently.*) What d'ye think of that?

MISS MOFFAT: No. Figures aren't his strong point.

THE SQUIRE: Thought you said he was clever.

MISS MOFFAT: To begin with, he can write.

THE SQUIRE: Oh. Well?

MISS MOFFAT: Very well.

THE SQUIRE: Then he could make fair copies. Eh?

MISS MOFFAT (*patiently*): No. (*Choosing her words carefully.*) This boy . . . is quite out of the ordinary.

THE SQUIRE: Sure?

MISS MOFFAT (*with great earnestness*): As sure as one of your miners would be, cutting through coal and striking a diamond without a flaw. He was born with very exceptional gifts. They must be—they ought to be given every chance.

THE SQUIRE: You mean he might turn into a literary bloke?

MISS MOFFAT: He might, yes.

THE SQUIRE: I'm blowed! How d'ye know?

MISS MOFFAT: By his work. It's very good.

THE SQUIRE: How d'ye know it's good?

MISS MOFFAT: How does one know Shakespeare's good?

THE SQUIRE: Shakespeare? What's he got to do with it?

MISS MOFFAT: He was a literary bloke.

THE SQUIRE: Ye-es. *He* was good, of course.

MISS MOFFAT: But how do you *know* he was?

THE SQUIRE (*after thought*): I've heard he was.

MISS MOFFAT: This little tenant of yours, Squire, has it in him to bring great credit to you.

THE SQUIRE: Yes, he *is* a tenant of mine, isn't he?

MISS MOFFAT: Imagine if you could say that you had known—well, say Lord Tennyson, as a boy on your estate!

THE SQUIRE: Rather a lark, what? (*Sobering.*) Though it's a bit different, y'know, Tennyson was at Cambridge. My old college.

MISS MOFFAT (*damped*): Oh . . . (*Rising and crossing towards her desk.*) Poor Evans. What a pity he was not born at the beginning of the eighteenth century!

THE SQUIRE (*pondering*): Beginning of the eighteenth century—now when was that . . .

MISS MOFFAT (*wandering to the bookshelves between the side window and the garden door*): He would have had a protector.

THE SQUIRE: What against?

MISS MOFFAT: A patron. (*Taking down two books and coming back to him.*) Pope, you recall, dedicated the famous "Essay on Man" to his protector. (*Showing him the flyleaf of the first book.*)

THE SQUIRE (*reading*): "To H. St. John Lord Bolingbroke." Mmm . . . I *have* heard of it, now I remember——

MISS MOFFAT: Isn't it wonderful to think that that inscription is handed down to posterity? (*Reading from the other book.*) "To the Right Honourable Earl of Southampton. . . . Your Honour's in all duty, William Shakespeare."

THE SQUIRE: Oh.

MISS MOFFAT: I often think of the pride that surged in the Earl's bosom when his encouragement gave birth to the masterpiece of a poor and humble writer!

THE SQUIRE: Funny, I never thought of Shakespeare being poor, somehow.

MISS MOFFAT: Some say his father was a butcher. The Earl realised he had genius, and fostered it.

THE SQUIRE: Mmm!

> *She takes the books and places them on the table, studying him anxiously behind his back.*

(*Following her reasoning with surprising quickness.*) If this boy really is clever, it seems a pity for *me* not to do something about it, doesn't it?

MISS MOFFAT (*eagerly*): A great pity. (*Sitting beside him, on his right this time, and mustering for the offensive.*) And I can tell you exactly how you can do something about it.

THE SQUIRE: How?

MISS MOFFAT: There's a scholarship going.

THE SQUIRE: Scholarship? Where?

Miss Moffat: To Oxford.

The Squire (*staggered*): Oxford?

Miss Moffat (*attacking hard*): A scholarship to Trinity College, Oxford, open to boys of secondary education in the British Isles. My school hardly comes under the heading of secondary education, and I wrote to your brother at Magdalen, he pulled some strings for me, and they have agreed to make a special case of this boy, on one condition. That you vouch for him. Will you?

The Squire: My dear lady, you take the cake. . . . Can't he be just as clever at home?

Miss Moffat: No, he can't. For the sort of future he ought to have, he must have polish—he has everything else. The background of a university would be invaluable to him. . . . Will you?

The Squire *blinks and rises. He is almost thinking.*

The Squire: Well, the 'Varsity, y'know, hang it all . . . mind you, he'll never get it.

Miss Moffat: I know, but he *must* have the chance——

The Squire: Still, y'know, even the mere prospect of one o' my miners——

Miss Moffat (*desperately*): Think of Shakespeare!

The Squire (*after a pause.*) All serene. (*As she rises.*) I'll drop a line to Henry next week. Rather a lark, what? I must be off——

Miss Moffat: I should be most obliged if the letter could be posted to-morrow. Would you like me to draft out a recommendation and send it over to the Hall? You must be so busy with the estate——

The Squire: I am rather. Polka supper to-morrow night. . . . Yes, do do that. (*Moving towards the front door.*) Good-bye, dear lady!

Miss Moffat (*seeing him out*): Thank you so very much, Squire——

The Squire: Happier conditions, and all that! Glad you've come to your senses!

Miss Moffat: Thank you so very much, Squire!

The Squire: Not at all, I'm all for giving a writer-fellow a helping hand. Tell my brother that, if you like. . . . (*At the front door.*) Y'know, I can never get over Henry bein' a Don, though I always said he'd end up as something funny . . .

> *He goes, chuckling. She shuts the door after him and walks down, relieved and excited.* MISS RONBERRY *hurries in from the garden, carrying the bowl of roses.*

MISS RONBERRY: Well?

MISS MOFFAT: That man is so stupid it sits on him like a halo.

MISS RONBERRY (*putting the bowl down on the desk, hurriedly*) What happened?

MISS MOFFAT: In ten minutes I have given the Squire the impression that he spends his whole time fostering genius in the illiterate.

MISS RONBERRY: But how?

MISS MOFFAT: Soft soap and curtseying; with my brain, my heart and my soul. I've beaten you at your own game, my dear, at my age and with my looks, I flirted with him! And he is going to write to Oxford; at least, I am going to write to Oxford for him. Hurray, hip, hip, hip, hip, hurray!

MISS RONBERRY: Oxford?

MISS MOFFAT (*shaking her, happily*): I am entering my little pit-pony for a scholarship to Oxford, child, Oxford University!

MISS RONBERRY (*incredulous*): But they don't have miners at Oxford University!

MISS MOFFAT: Well, they're going to. (*Haranguing her.*) The lad is on this earth for eighty years at the most out of a few millions, let the proud silly ones grovel and be useful for a change, so he can step up on their backs to something better! I was bursting to say that to the Lord of the Manor, so I must vent it on you. . . . Thank you for your shawl, my dear—(*wrapping it round the helpless* MISS RONBERRY *and piloting her to the front door*)—and now you've served your purpose, you can go home—but you'd better watch out, I may race you to the altar yet——

> *She shuts the front door on her, and comes back into the room. She looks round, with a sigh of pleasure, then calls:*

Evans!

*She pulls the table round the sofa to the centre of the room,
takes the milk-jug and cup from the table to the desk, pulls the
desk-chair up to the table, and sits at it, studying the exercise-book
she has been correcting earlier. She holds her eyes a moment; it is
obvious that she could be tired if she allowed herself to be.*

MORGAN *comes in from the study, carrying a pen, books and
papers; his mantle of reserve has descended on him again; his inward
rebellion is only to be guessed at from his eyes, which she does not
see. He pulls the table-chair up to the table and sits opposite her,
half behind the sofa; it is apparent that this is a daily procedure
at this hour. He makes fitful notes of her ensuing comments. The
daylight begins to wane.*

Is this your essay on the Wealth of Nations?

MORGAN: Yes.

MISS MOFFAT (*reading briskly*): Say so and underline it. Nothing
irritates examiners more than that sort of vagueness.

*She crosses out three lines with a flourish, reads further, then
hands him the exercise-book.*

I couldn't work this sentence out.

MORGAN (*reading*): "The eighteenth century was a cauldron.
Vice and elegance boiled to a simmer until the kitchen of society
reeked fulminously, and the smell percolated to the marble halls
above."

MISS MOFFAT (*as he hands the book back to her*): D'ye know what
that means?

MORGAN: Yes, Miss Moffat.

MISS MOFFAT: Because I don't. Clarify, my boy, clarify, and
leave the rest to Mrs. Henry Wood. . . . "Water" with two t's
. . . (*scoring heavily*) . . . that's a bad lapse. . . . (*After reading
quickly to herself while he broods.*) The Adam Smith sentence was
good. Original, and clear as well. (*Writing.*) Seven out of ten,
not bad but not good—you *must* avoid long words until you
know exactly what they mean. Otherwise domino. . . . (*Handing
the essay back to him.*) Your reading?

MORGAN (*concentrating with an effort*): Burke's "Cause of the
Present Discontents".

MISS MOFFAT: Style?

MORGAN: His style appears to me . . . as if there was too much of it.

MISS MOFFAT (*mechanically*): His style struck me as florid.

MORGAN (*repeating*): "His style struck me as florid."

MISS MOFFAT: Again.

MORGAN (*mumbling*): "His style struck me as florid."

MISS MOFFAT: Subject matter?

MORGAN: A sound argument, falsified by—by the high colour of the sentiments.

MISS MOFFAT: Mmmm. "The high colour of the sentiments" . . . odd but not too odd, good and stylish. . . . For next time. (*Dictating, as* MORGAN *writes.*) Walpole and Sheridan as representatives of their age; and no smelly cauldrons. (*Opening another book.*) By the way, next Tuesday I'm starting you on Greek.

MORGAN (*looking up, feigning interest*): Oh yes?

    He writes again.

MISS MOFFAT (*subduing her excitement*): I am going to put you in for a scholarship to Oxford.

    A pause. He looks up at her, arrested.

MORGAN: Oxford? Where the lords go?

MISS MOFFAT (*amused*): The same. (*Rising happily, and crossing to the desk with the two books with which she wooed the* SQUIRE.) I've made a simplified alphabet to begin with. It's jolly interesting after Latin . . .

    She searches among her papers. The matter of factness with which she is (typically) controlling her excitement over the scholarship seems to gall him more and more; he watches her, bitterly.

Have a look at it by Tuesday, so we can make a good start—oh, and before we go on with the lesson, I've found the nail-file I mentioned——

    In his mood, this is the last straw. He flings his pen savagely down on the table.

(*Without noticing, rummaging briskly.*) I'll show you how to use it. I had them both here somewhere——

MORGAN (*quietly*): I shall not need a nail-file in the coal-mine.

MISS MOFFAT (*mechanically, still intent at the desk*): In the what?

MORGAN: I am going back to the coal-mine.

She turns and looks at him. He rises, breathing fast. They look at each other. A pause.

MISS MOFFAT (*perplexed*): I don't understand you. Explain yourself.

MORGAN: I do not want to learn Greek, nor to pronounce any long English words, nor to keep my hands clean.

MISS MOFFAT (*staggered*): What's the matter with you? Why not?

MORGAN: Because . . . (*plunging*) . . . because I was born in a Welsh hayfield when my mother was helpin' with the harvest— and I always lived in a little house with no stairs only a ladder— and no water—and until my brothers was killed I never sleep except three in a bed. I know that is terrible grammar but it is true.

MISS MOFFAT: What on earth has three in a bed got to do with learning Greek?

MORGAN: It has—a lot! The last two years I have not had no proper talk with English chaps in the mine because I was so busy keepin' this old grammar in its place. Tryin' to better myself . . . (*his voice rising*) . . . tryin' to better myself, the day and the night! . . . You cannot take a nail-file into the "Gwesmor Arms" public bar!

MISS MOFFAT: My dear boy, file your nails at home! I never heard anything so ridiculous. Besides, you don't go to the Gwesmor Arms!

MORGAN: Yes I do, I have been there every afternoon for a week, spendin' your pocket-money, and I have been there now, and that is why I can speak my mind!

She looks at him, alarmed and puzzled.

MISS MOFFAT: I had no idea that you felt like this.

MORGAN: Because you are not interested in me.

MISS MOFFAT (*incredulously*): Not interested in you?

MORGAN (*losing control*): How can you be interested in a machine that you put a penny in and if nothing comes out you give it a good shake? "Evans, write me an essay, Evans, get up and bow, Evans, what is a subjunctive"! My name is Morgan Evans, and all my friends call me Morgan, and if there is anything gets on the wrong side of me it is callin' me Evans! . . . And do you know what they call me in the village? Ci bach yr ysgol! The schoolmistress's little dog. What has it got to do with you if my nails are dirty? Mind your own business!

He bursts into sobs and buries his head in his hands on the end of the sofa.

She turns away from him, instinctively shying from the spectacle of his grief. A pause. She is extremely upset, but tries hard not to show it. She waits for him to recover, and takes a step towards him.

MISS MOFFAT: I never meant you to know this. I have spent money on you—(*as he winces quickly*)—I don't mind that, money ought to be spent. But time is different. Your life has not yet begun, mine is half over. And when you're a middle-aged spinster, some folk say it's pretty near finished. Two years is valuable currency. I have spent two years on you. (*As he raises his head and stares before him, trying not to listen to her.*) Ever since that first day, the mainspring of this school has been your career. Sometimes, in the middle of the night, when I have been desperately tired, I have lain awake, making plans. Large and small. Sensible and silly. Plans, for you. And you tell me I have no interest in you. If I say any more I shall start to cry; and I haven't cried since I was younger than you are, and I'd never forgive you for that. (*Walking brusquely to the front door and throwing on her cloak.*) I am going for a walk. I don't like this sort of conversation, please never mention it again. If you want to go on, be at school to-morrow. (*Going.*) If not, don't.

MORGAN (*muttering, fiercely*): I don't want your money, and I don't want your time! . . . I don't want to be thankful to no strange woman—for anything!

A pause.

MISS MOFFAT (*shaking her head, helplessly*): I don't understand you. I don't understand you at all.

She goes out by the front door.

He sits up and folds his arms, with a deep breath; he feels something in his breast pocket, roots out a little rum bottle, takes a pull at it, lifts an exercise-book, crashes it viciously on the table, and

60

relapses into moody thought. The daylight has faded perceptibly. Without his hearing her, BESSIE *comes in from the garden. She has put her hair half up and wears ear-rings.*

BESSIE: Hello!

    He stares at her coldly, plants the bottle on the table and stares away again.

(*She clutches her leg, ostentatiously.*) Caught my knee climbin' down the rainpipe, ooh . . . (*As he takes no notice.*) P'r'aps I'm invisible . . .

    She tosses her head, marches into the kitchen, singing raucously, and bangs the door behind her. Far away, the sound of singing: men returning from the mine, harmonising their familiar melody, "Yr Hufen Melyn". MORGAN *brushes a tear angrily from his cheek, but unhappy thoughts assail him; his mood is fed by the music. A pause.* BESSIE *returns from the kitchen. She is suddenly changed, subdued and almost timid.*

BESSIE: Mum's gone out. (*After a pause, advancing slowly towards the foot of the stairs.*) Expect she's gone to tell Mrs. Roberts about her meetin'. Though how she manages with Mrs. Roberts knowin' no English an' deaf as well . . . (*After a pause.*) Talking a lot, aren't I?

MORGAN: Yes.

BESSIE: Well, *I'm* not deaf.

MORGAN (*looking up at her*): Been spyin'?

BESSIE (*pointing upstairs*): If people lock me in and take the key out of the key-hole, they can't blame me for listenin' at it. (*As he turns away.*) Oo, I think she's wicked.

MORGAN (*stung*): Mind your own business!

BESSIE: I won't. (*Gaining confidence.*) I like to know about everything. I like doin' all the things I like, I like sweets, I don't care if it does make me fat, and I *love* ear-rings. I like to shake my head like a lady. . . .

    She stands, hands on hips, transformed from the sullen child into something crafty, mischievous and attractive.

    The singing stops. A pause.

It's funny. . . . We never been by ourselves before.

    He looks at her. She returns the look. He turns away, disconsolate.

A pause. She wanders up towards the bay window, and begins to sing in Welsh, in a voice surprisingly pure and pleasing. The tune is "Lliw Gwyn Rhosyn yr Haf". He raises his head and listens, arrested. She leans against one of the desks in the window recess, and looks out towards the setting sun; her voice ends softly on a phrase. A pause. She turns her head and looks at him. She smiles, begins to sing again, more sure of herself, and walks slowly between the desks to his right, where she rests her elbows deliberately on the table with a deliberate movement; she looks dreamily before her as her voice dies away. He looks sharply round at her. Slowly her head turns towards him; slowly she smiles at him; subtle, and quite self-confident now.

BESSIE: Didn't know I knew Welsh, did you? . . . You like that song, don't you? That's why I learnt it.

MORGAN: You are different when you sing.

BESSIE: Am I? . . . (*Picking the bottle from the table.*) What's this, medicine? (*Taking a gulp, and choking.*) Tastes like rubber. Nice though . . . (*As he takes it roughly from her, rises, drains the bottle, and puts it back in his pocket.*) You know, you was quite right to put her in her place. Clever chap like you learnin' lessons off a woman!

MORGAN: That's right . . .

BESSIE (*soft, persuasive*): You don't 'ave to go to Oxford! Clever chap like you!

MORGAN (*in a whisper*): That's right . . .

He turns slowly and looks at her. She crosses behind him and sits on the back of the sofa.

BESSIE: What a man wants is a bit o' sympathy!

He looks at her, his hand on the back of the chair. It is growing faintly darker. She laughs, and begins to sing again; she turns, still singing, looks up at him, and smiles. He pushes away the chair, seizes her with violence, and kisses her passionately. Their arms entwine and the chair crashes to the floor.

Black out. The curtain falls, and rises immediately on

Scene II

A morning in November, three months later. The room is much as it was; the potted plants have been removed; the daylight is so poor that the lamps are lit.

MRS. WATTY *is carrying in from the kitchen a small table, new and light, with on it blotter, ink, pens, pencil, a duster and a cup of tea.* MISS RONBERRY *is pushing the armchair in from the study past the sofa into its old place, next to the isolated desk.*

MRS. WATTY (*singing*): I'm saved I am, I'm saved I am . . .

She puts down the small table, pushes the desk-chair back against the desk, drags the large table and its chair to its old place behind the sofa, then sets the small table well downstage, between the armchair and the sofa. She fetches a loose seat attached to one of the desks and places it below the small table, its back to the audience. (*During this.*) What would the armchair be for, miss?

MISS RONBERRY: The Squire's coming. He's invigilating.

MRS. WATTY: *What* was that, please, miss?

MISS RONBERRY (*taking a parcel tied with string from a drawer in the desk, and unpacking papers from it*): The Oxford people have appointed him and Miss Moffat to watch Morgan Evans while he is sitting the scholarship, so that he cannot cheat.

MRS. WATTY: What a shame . . . (*Still arranging furniture.*) You'd never think it was nearly nine in the morning, would you?

MISS RONBERRY (*peering out of the side window*): It's stopped snowing.

MRS. WATTY: Only just. The milkman said the road was blocked down by the bridge.

MISS RONBERRY: How terrible if Morgan couldn't get through!

MRS. WATTY: Countin' sheep all night, I was. She didn't 'ave a wink neither. (*Picking up two envelopes from the floor, near the front door.*) I could 'ear her thinkin'.

MISS RONBERRY: It is a very important day for her.

MRS. WATTY (*handing the envelopes to her*): Looks like that one's Bessie. Would you mind?

MISS RONBERRY (*opening it*): That means Sarah the Post got through——

MRS. WATTY: She'd come the other way, down the 'ill——

MISS RONBERRY: That's true . . . (*Reading.*) "Dear Mum"—to think I taught her to write—"Cheltenham is terrible. Can I have a shilling. I do the steps. Madam is terrible. Your obedient girl."

MRS. WATTY (*taking back the letter, as* MISS RONBERRY *glances at the other and tucks it into her belt*): Obedient, I like that . . · (*Throwing the letter into the waste-paper-basket.*) She's been away three months now, she ought to be gettin' used to it.

MISS RONBERRY (*busy at the desk*): But do you not miss her?

MRS. WATTY (*emphatically, dusting the little table*): No! I don't like 'er, you know, never 'ave.

MISS RONBERRY: But Mrs. Watty, your own daughter!

MRS. WATTY: I know, but I've never been able to take to 'er. First time I saw 'er, I said "No". (*Going.*) With 'er dad being foreign, you see.

MISS RONBERRY: But couldn't your husband have taken her abroad to his own family?

MRS. WATTY: Oh, my 'usband was quite different. British to the core.

> She goes into the kitchen. MISS RONBERRY *blinks after her, and places foolscap paper on the little table.* MISS MOFFAT *comes slowly downstairs. She is alert, but more subdued than the audience has yet seen her.* MISS RONBERRY *takes up the cup of tea, and watches her, apprehensively, as she crosses her.*

MISS MOFFAT: It's stopped snowing.

MISS RONBERRY (*sitting on the sofa, and sipping*): It's a white world, as they say . . . (*Watching* MISS MOFFAT *as she looks out of the side window.*) Do you think he will get through the snow?

MISS MOFFAT: This morning he would get through anything.

MISS RONBERRY: I am so glad. I thought perhaps he—he had not been working satisfactorily——

MISS MOFFAT: At ten o'clock last night I had to take his books away from him.

MISS RONBERRY: I *am* glad.

MISS MOFFAT (*still looking out*): I hope he won't get wet—he must not be upset in any way . . . (*Playing nervously with the string MISS RONBERRY has left on the desk.*) What made you think he wasn't working well?

MISS RONBERRY (*flustered*): Nothing, only . . . you remember the night you went for that long walk, when he might be going back to the mine?

MISS MOFFAT (*after a pause*): Yes?

MISS RONBERRY: The next morning he started studying again, and yet it seemed so different.

MISS MOFFAT: How?

MISS RONBERRY: Almost strained . . . what a silly thing to say . . . I mean, as you did not say anything more about the mine——

MISS MOFFAT (*playing with the string*): He didn't say any more himself. He just turned up. I didn't embrace him on both cheeks, but I said "righto". Since which time, he has never stopped working.

MISS RONBERRY: I *am* so glad . . . (*Taking the other envelope from her belt, relieved to be changing the subject.*) Oh, this arrived from the Penlan Town Hall! It must be his birth certificate——

MISS MOFFAT: Good . . . (*Crossing, taking it from her briskly, and taking it back to her desk.*) I must send it off to the President of Trinity. Rather a nervous post-mortem from him last night; two pages to ask if the youngster's legitimate; thank Heaven he is. And no convictions for drunkenness; references have been spotless. That will help, I hope.

MISS RONBERRY: Would it not be splendid if he . . . won!

MISS MOFFAT (*after a pause*): Not very likely, I am afraid. (*Moving about, nervously.*) The syllabus rather attaches importance to general knowledge of the academic sort. His is bound to be patchy —on the exuberant side—I have had to force it; two years is not enough even for him. If he checks himself, and does not start telling them what they ought to think of Milton, with fair luck he might stand a chance. He will have some pretty strong public-school candidates against him, of course. Bound to. It depends on how much the examiners will appreciate a highly original intelligence.

MISS RONBERRY: But wouldn't it be *exciting!*

MISS MOFFAT (*after a pause, in a measured voice*): Yes, it would. People run down the Universities, and always will, but it would be a wonderful thing for him. It would be a wonderful thing for rural education all over the country.

MISS RONBERRY: And most of all, it would be a wonderful thing for you!

MISS MOFFAT: I suppose so . . . (*After a pause, almost soliloquising.*) It is odd to have spent so many hours with another human being, in the closest intellectual communion—because it has been that, I know every trick and twist of that brain of his, exactly where it will falter and where it will gallop ahead of me—and yet not to know him at all. (*Realising the other woman's presence, and breaking her mood.*) I woke up in the middle of the night thinking of Henry the Eighth. I have a feeling there may be a question about the old boy and the Papacy. (*At one of the bookshelves between the side window and the garden door.*) I'll cram one or two facts into him, the last minute . . . (*Suddenly, in a sob, with all the inward strength of which she is capable.*) Oh God, he must win it . . .

> MRS. WATTY *comes in from the kitchen, carrying a steaming cup and saucer.*

(*Leaning her head against the bookcase; brokenly.*) He must . . .

> MRS. WATTY *stops short, and exchanges a distressed look with* MISS RONBERRY. *She goes over to* MISS MOFFAT.

MRS. WATTY (*coaxingly*): Tea!

> MISS MOFFAT *turns and looks at her, trying to pull herself together.*

(*Giving her the tea-cup and stirring the tea for her, with an attempt at jauntiness.*) Now, ma'am, don't get in a pucker! Six more Saturday mornin's like this in the next 'alf-year, remember!

MISS MOFFAT (*recovering quickly, and making a note at the desk, from a book*): The first paper is the important one—I expect we'll get more used to the others——

MISS RONBERRY (*chatty again, as* MRS. WATTY *takes the empty cup*): Suppose the Squire doesn't come!

MISS MOFFAT: He will. He has got to the point of looking on the lad as a race-horse.

MISS RONBERRY: You don't think the snow might deter him?

MRS. WATTY: I just seed 'is nibs' gardener clearin' a way from the gates. Shame the red carpet gettin' so wet.

She goes back into the kitchen. MISS RONBERRY rises and looks out of the side window.

MISS RONBERRY: Surely it is getting brighter this side . . . Oh, I can see him! Morgan, I mean!

MISS MOFFAT (*looking past her*): Can you?

MISS RONBERRY: Coming up the Nant, do you see? Ploughing through!

MISS MOFFAT: What is the time?

MISS RONBERRY: Ten minutes to!

MISS MOFFAT (*sitting at her desk and searching again in her book*): He will have just two minutes——

A knock at the front door.

MISS MOFFAT: Good. There's the Squire——

MISS RONBERRY (*running to the front door*): He is as excited as any of us——

She opens the front door. BESSIE stands in the porch, in the drifted snow. She enters the room, followed by MR. JONES, heavily muffled and looking very sheepish. MISS RONBERRY shuts the door and follows them into the room in wonderment. They are faintly powdered with snow.

Bessie! . . . But it cannot be you, your mother has just received——

BESSIE: I left the same day I posted it.

She is shabbily dressed, in semi-grown up fashion, and wears a cloak. Her manner is staccato, nervy and defiant; she is bursting with news, which might be good or bad. Her hands twitching over her Gladstone bag, she faces MISS MOFFAT, who stares at her, puzzled.

MISS MOFFAT (*without rising*): This is unexpected.

BESSIE: Isn't it just? I have been travellin' all night, quite a wreck. I woke Mr. Jones up and he got the station-master to drive us over in his trap, in the snow, nice, wasn't it?

She is trying not to be frightened, and not succeeding. The conversation from now on quickens and grows more nervous.

MISS MOFFAT: You have arrived at an inconvenient time.

BESSIE: Fancy.

She plucks up courage and sits suddenly in the armchair. MISS MOFFAT *frowns and rises.* MISS RONBERRY *is near the kitchen door;* MR. JONES *hovers round the front door.*

MISS MOFFAT: Have you come to see your mother?

BESSIE: No.

MISS MOFFAT: Then why are you here?

BESSIE: Questions and answers, just like school again!

MISS MOFFAT (*to* MR. JONES): Why have you brought this girl here this morning?

MR. JONES: I did not bring her, Miss Moffat, she brought me——

MISS MOFFAT (*to* BESSIE): Whom have you come to see?

BESSIE: You.

MISS MOFFAT: Me?

BESSIE *does not speak. Undecided,* MISS MOFFAT *crosses above the armchair, looks at the clock, then quickly out of the side window.*

I can give you exactly one minute of my time. Is it money? (*As* BESSIE *does not answer, impatiently to the others.*) Will you wait in the study?

MR. JONES *follows* MISS RONBERRY *into the study; she is perplexed, he is very worried.*

MISS MOFFAT (*before they are out of the room*): One minute . . . Quickly!

BESSIE: Why?

MISS MOFFAT: Morgan Evans is sitting for his Oxford examination here this morning.

BESSIE: Well, 'e needn't.

MISS MOFFAT: What do you mean?

BESSIE: Because he won't ever be goin' to Oxford.

MISS MOFFAT: Why not?

BESSIE: Because there's goin' to be a little stranger.

A pause.

I'm going to have a little stranger.

She begins to whimper into her handkerchief; half acting, half nerves and excitement. MISS MOFFAT *stares at her.*

MISS MOFFAT: You're lying.

BESSIE (*looking up, suddenly*): Doctor Brett, The Firs, Cheltenham . . . And if you don't believe it's Morgan Evans, you ask 'im about that night you locked me up—the night you had the words with him!

A pause.

MISS MOFFAT: I see . . . (*With a sudden cry.*) Why couldn't I have seen before! . . .

Her eyes rest on the examination table. She collects herself, desperately.

Does he know?

BESSIE: I've come to tell 'im! I was ever so upset, of course, and now I've lost me place—ooh, she was artful—he'll have to marry me, or I'll show him up, 'cause I must give the little stranger a name——

MISS MOFFAT (*exasperated beyond endurance*): Stop saying "little stranger", if you must have a baby, then call it a baby! . . . Have you told anybody?

BESSIE: Mr. Jones, that's all——

MISS RONBERRY *peers timidly round the study door.*

MISS RONBERRY: The Squire is coming up the road!

She looks anxiously from one to the other and goes back into the study.

BESSIE: I'll wait here for him.

MISS MOFFAT (*panting*): For the next three hours, he must not be disturbed. You are not going to see him——

BESSIE (*almost triumphantly*): You can't bully me, the way I am! (*Rising, and facing her across the examination table, the resentment of two years pouring out, real hysteria this time.*) 'Asn't sunk in yet, 'as it? I'm teaching *you* something, am I? You didn't know things like that went on, did you? Why? You couldn't see what was goin' on under your nose, 'cause you're too busy managin' everythin'! Well, you can't manage him any longer, 'cause he's got to manage me now, the way I am, he's got to——

MR. JONES *pokes his head round the study door; he is in a state of panic.* MISS RONBERRY *hovers behind him.*

MR. JONES: Morgan Evans has turned the corner up the hill——

MISS RONBERRY: So there isn't much time!

MR. JONES *gives the others a desperate look and follows* MISS RONBERRY *back into the study.*

MISS MOFFAT: I'm afraid I am going to do a little managing now. You are going into the kitchen, where your mother will make you breakfast; you will then lie down, and as soon as this session is finished we will go upstairs and talk it all over when we are a little calmer.

A knock at the front door.

BESSIE : He's here! (*Rising.*) I got to see him!

MISS MOFFAT (*seizing her by the arm, suddenly*): If you try and disobey me, I shall not answer for the consequences.

BESSIE (*cowed*): You wouldn't dare lay a finger on me——

MISS MOFFAT: Oh yes, I would.

They face each other, panting; deadly enemies.

MISS MOFFAT: If you attempt to stay in this room, or to blab to anybody about this before we have had that talk—even your mother—I am in a pretty nervous state myself, this morning, and I shall strike you so hard that I shall probably kill you, and be hanged as a thwarted spinster . . . I mean every word of that.

Another knock, more impatient. She quells BESSIE *with her look; crosses, and holds open the kitchen door.*

BESSIE: I don't mind. (*Following her, and turning at the door.*) Three hours'll go soon enough.

She goes into the kitchen, her head high. MISS MOFFAT *shuts the door after her, straightens herself, and opens the front door. The* SQUIRE *enters, in Inverness cape and hat, stamping the snow from his boots; he carries several periodicals, chiefly* Sporting and Dramatic. *The rest of the scene is played very quickly.*

MISS MOFFAT (*shutting the door*): So very sorry—how kind of you—such a dreadful day——

THE SQUIRE: Not at all, Mistress Pedagogue, anything for a lark . . . (*Looking at the little table.*) Glad it isn't me, what? . . .

(*Settling on the sofa, as she takes his overcoat.*) I've got a spiffy bit of news for you.

MISS MOFFAT: Yes?

THE SQUIRE: I've bought the barn from Sir Herbert, and we can move the whole shoot next door by March. What d'ye think?

MISS MOFFAT (*abstracted, hanging the coat behind the front door*): Wonderful——

THE SQUIRE (*showing the study as he settles on the sofa*): We can knock a door straight through here to the barn——

> *A knock at the front door.*

Aren't ye pleased about it?

MISS MOFFAT (*crossing to the desk, hardly aware of what she is doing, as* MISS RONBERRY *runs in from the study*): Yes, but you know, this examination, rather worrying——

MISS RONBERRY (*crossing*): Good morning, Squire! Terrible weather——

THE SQUIRE (*half rising*): Beastly——

> MISS RONBERRY *opens the front door and lets* MORGAN *in. His overcoat, cap and muffler are sprinkled with snow. He has been hurrying, but he is quiet and calm. His eyes rest immediately on the little examination table.*

MISS MOFFAT: Wet?

MORGAN (*taking off his overcoat*): No, thank you—good-day, sir——

MISS RONBERRY: Let me take your things——

MORGAN: Thank you——

MISS MOFFAT: Before I open the papers, I have a feeling they may bring up Henry the Eighth. (*Holding out the paper on which she has been scribbling.*) Memorise these two facts, will you?

> MORGAN *takes the paper and studies it, brushing stray flakes of snow out of his hair as he does so.*

MISS RONBERRY (*taking a spray from her blouse and laying it on the small table*): White heather—just a thought!

> *She runs into the study with* MORGAN'S *coat, scarf and cap.*

MORGAN: Thank you——

THE SQUIRE: Good luck, my boy.

MORGAN: Thank you, sir——

THE SQUIRE: Glad it isn't me!

MR. JONES *pops his head round the study door.*

MR. JONES: Pob llwyddiant, ymachgeni!

MORGAN: Diolch——

MR. JONES *goes back into the study.* MORGAN *hands the paper back to* MISS MOFFAT, *who crumples it and throws it in the waste-paper-basket. He sits at the little table, his back to the audience.*

MISS MOFFAT: Name and particulars, to save time. And don't get exuberant.

MORGAN: No.

MISS MOFFAT: Or illegible.

MORGAN: No.

He writes. She takes up an official envelope from the desk.

THE SQUIRE: But aren't *you* going to wish my little protégé good fortune?

MISS MOFFAT (*after a pause, to* MORGAN): Good luck.

MORGAN (*looking up at her, after a pause*): Thank you.

The clock begins to strike nine.

MISS MOFFAT: Ready?

MORGAN *nods. She cuts the envelope and places the examination paper in front of him. He studies it anxiously. She looks at the duplicate.*

(*Involuntarily, gratified.*) Henry the Eighth!

She sits in the armchair. The SQUIRE *embarks on his periodical.* MORGAN *begins to write.* MISS MOFFAT *raises her head, looks anxiously towards the kitchen, then steadfastly at* MORGAN, *her lip trembling. A pause. The only sound is the scratch of a pen.*

THE CURTAIN FALLS SLOWLY

ACT III

An afternoon in July. Seven months later.

 The school has been moved next door, and the room is much less crowded; the small table is back in the window recess, the armchair is in its old position; the large table, however, is no longer behind the sofa with its chair, its place being taken by three small school-desks facing the front door; between the front door and the bay window a blackboard on its easel faces the audience at an angle, with "Elizabeth, known as Good Q. Bess" written on it in block letters.

 MR. JONES *stands in command beside the blackboard. In two of the school-desks sit* IDWAL *and* ROBBART, *each poring over his slate. On the settle sit* THE SQUIRE, *downstage, his arms folded like a pupil, his eyes fixed on* MR. JONES, *and next to him* OLD TOM, *upstage, laboriously copying the inscription on to his slate.*

OLD TOM (*muttering, as he writes*): Elissabeth . . . known . . . as . . . what in goodness is a "k" doin' there, that iss a pussell for me——

MR. JONES (*suddenly*): "I wandered lonely as a cloud." From the Daffodils, by Wordsworth.

 The boys scratch busily. THE SQUIRE *begins to nod sleepily.*

 MISS RONBERRY *hurries in from the garden.*

MISS RONBERRY (*to* MR. JONES, *in an urgent whisper*): What is the capital of Sweden?

MR. JONES: Stockholm.

MISS RONBERRY: Thank you.

 She hurries back into the garden.

OLD TOM (*after pondering anxiously, to* THE SQUIRE): Please, sir, how many l's in "daffodils"?

THE SQUIRE: Blest if I know.

 He closes his eyes again. JOHN OWEN *comes in by the study door.*

JOHN: Please, Mistar Jones, Form Two Arithmetic Report—Miss Moffat says will you come in school with it.

He goes back. MR. JONES *takes some papers hastily from the dresser and follows him through the study. A mild snore from* THE SQUIRE.

ROBBART (*looking at him*): Mae o'n cysgu. Tyd. Idwal——

OLD TOM (*in a passion*): Plenty Welsh at home, not in the class please by request scoundrels and notty boys!

IDWAL (*to him*): Squire iss 'avin' a snore. Nai ddangos rwbeth ichi——

He rises, runs to the blackboard, takes the chalk and the duster, and swiftly rubs out and adds to the inscription till it reads: "NO . . . GOOD . . . BESSIE." THE SQUIRE *grunts.* IDWAL *throws the duster under the open desk, darts back to his desk and buries his head in his slate.* MR. JONES *returns.*

MR. JONES: Now history. (*Crossing* THE SQUIRE, *waking him.*) Excuse me . . . (*Going to the blackboard.*) Elizabeth——

He sees the inscription and stops short. He turns on the others, grave and perturbed. OLD TOM *watches, missing nothing.*
Who did this?

IDWAL: Please, Mr. Jones, perhaps it iss some terrible dunce that want to know what iss Bessie Watty been doin' the last few months.

A pause.

MR. JONES: Whoever it was . . . I am going to cane him! (*To* THE SQUIRE, *timidly, as the latter rises and walks up.*) It was not you, sir, by any chance?

THE SQUIRE: Not guilty . . . (*Going to the bay window and peering out towards the left.*) Bessie Watty? Little Cockney thing? Nice ankles?

MR. JONES: I do not know, sir . . . (*As* IDWAL *giggles.*) Silence, boys! Where is my duster?

THE SQUIRE (*coming back with a sigh*): Still no sign of him.

MR. JONES: You mean Morgan Evans, sir?

The boys sober suddenly and look round at THE SQUIRE.
He is not expected before the train leaving Oxford half-past one——

THE SQUIRE: There's a sporting chance the Viva finished yesterday, and I sent the wagonette to meet the one-ten.

He sits again on the settle. The boys watch him.

Mr. Jones: Do you think that he may know the result when he arrives?

The Squire: I doubt it, Miss Moffat said we'll hear by letter in a day or two . . . (*Rising restlessly, and going towards the front door.*) Think I'll propel the old pins down the highway, just in case . . .

Idwal: Please, sir, what sort of a place is Oxford?

The Squire (*turning at the door*): Dunno, I'm sure. Cambridge myself.

He goes.

Mr. Jones (*standing in front of the blackboard*): Now history. Repeat after me——

Idwal (*in a piping voice*): Please, Mr. Jones, tell us about Bessie Watty!

Mr. Jones (*after a pause, cornered*): If you are kept in to-morrow, I will give you religion. Repeat after me——

The school bell rings.

Dismiss!

He goes to the dresser and tidies papers in his satchel. Idwal *and* Robbart *breathe on their slates and wipe them, gather their books hurriedly together and tie them with a strap.* Sarah *hurries in from the front door. She is dressed in her best, in the traditional Welsh peasant costume with a steeple hat.*

Sarah: Please, sir, have you got my father——(*Seeing* Old Tom.)—tiddona, n'had, ma'dy frwas di'n oeri——

Old Tom (*furious*): English, daughter, in the class, pliss!

Sarah (*pulling at his Sleeve*): You are an old soft, your porridge it iss gettin' cold and you have not got your sleep——

Old Tom: But I got my Queen Elizabeth——

Sarah (*helping him towards the front door*): And in the mornin' you got your rheumatics—come on!

Miss Ronberry *comes in from the garden and places her papers on the open desk.*

Robbart: Sarah Pugh, what you all clobbered up for?

Sarah: Because for Morgan Evans.

Mr. Jones (*starting forward*): Is there some news?

Miss Ronberry: About Morgan? Oh, quickly!

Sarah: Not yet, Mistar Jones. (*As they sigh impatiently.*) But when it comes, I know it iss good news, so what do I do` I open the dresser, out the lavendar bags and into my Sundays! Home, dada, for Sundays——

MR. JONES: Before we have definite news, that is unwise——

SARAH: John Goronwy Jones pliss sir, you are an old soft. Everybody is ready to meet him by the Nant! The grocer got his fiddle——

IDWAL: And William Williams the public got his cornet!

ROBBART: And with me on me mouth-organ——

SARAH: And me singin'!

ROBBART: Tyd, Idwal——

He runs out by the front door, followed by IDWAL.

MR. JONES (*calling after them*): Jack Rhys Policeman will be after you with his breach of the peace!

MISS RONBERRY: Perhaps preparing for news to be good means that it will be.

MR. JONES: Everything is pre-ordained. Morgan Evans has either won the scholarship, or lost it.

MISS RONBERRY: Let us all say together, "Morgan Evans has won the scholarship"!

ALL (*except* MR. JONES, *lustily*): "Morgan Evans has won the scholarship!"

SARAH (*to* OLD TOM): Tiddona, 'nhad——

She stands arranging her shawl.

OLD TOM (*wistfully*): I never got a lettar yet, and nobody never put Sundays on for me . . .

He goes out by the front door. MISS RONBERRY *is about to cross into the school when her eye catches the blackboard;* SARAH *is about to follow her father when* MISS RONBERRY'S *voice arrests her.*

MISS RONBERRY: "No . . . good . . . Bessie." Good gracious!

MR. JONES (*trying to hide the board from* SARAH, *but too late*): Where *is* my duster?

MISS RONBERRY: What does that mean?

SARAH: Bessie Watty. Miss Ronberry, where is she?

MISS RONBERRY (*after a stifled look at* MR. JONES): I don't know, dear.

76

SARAH: Miss Moffat she hears from her, in my post-office. We wass all wonderin'.

She goes out by the front door.

MISS RONBERRY (*turning on* MR. JONES): Well, *I* have been wondering too! (*Sitting on the sofa, as he crosses to the desk.*) She came back that morning and just went away again—Morgan Evans was telling me only the day he left for Oxford that he didn't even *see* her. Where is she?

MR. JONES (*pouring ink from a bottle in a drawer into a rack of inkwells on the desk*): It is more important to know if Morgan Evans has won or not.

MISS RONBERRY: I know . . . If he hasn't, it will break her heart.

MR. JONES: Would she feel it so keen as all that?

MISS RONBERRY: I used not to think so, but since that day they have been so much better friends, it has been a pleasure to hear them conversing—perhaps it is the strain of all these examinations——

She stops guiltily as MISS MOFFAT *comes in from the study, reading an exercise-book and chuckling; she wanders up towards the blackboard.*

MISS MOFFAT: Gwyneth Thomas the plasterer's eldest: essay on Knowledge. "Be good, sweet maid, and let who will be clever"—I wonder if the reverend Kingsley had any idea what a smack in the eye that was for lady teachers? And then Gwyneth Thomas starts (*reading*) "It is not nice to know too much, I wish to be like Miss Ronberry, Miss Moffat is different, she knows everything." Ha! Not bad for a youngster! Hit the nail—— (*Suddenly, apprehensively, catching* MISS RONBERRY'S *face*.) Any news?

MR. JONES: Not yet.

MISS MOFFAT (*relieved*): I thought not . . .

She sees the blackboard and stops short. A pause. She takes out her handkerchief and with a swift movement wipes the board clean. The others watch her.

Where is the Squire?

MR. JONES: Gone to see if there is any sign.

MISS MOFFAT: Thank the Lord, that man is really becoming

77

a nuisance. (*Sitting on the top end of the sofa.*) He gave up Henley to be here this week—did you know?

MR. JONES (*coming down towards her*): You do not appear nervous?

MISS MOFFAT: I am past being nervous. If he has won, I shan't believe it. Flatly.

MISS RONBERRY: And if he has lost?

MISS MOFFAT: If he has lost . . . (*after a pause*) . . . we must proceed as if nothing had happened. The sun rises and sets every day, and while it does we have jolly well got to revolve round it; the time to sit up and take notice will be the day it decides not to appear. (*Rising briskly.*) In the meantime, Mr. Jones, your report is on your desk; Miss Ronberry, Form Two are waiting for your music like a jungle of hungry parakeets.

MISS RONBERRY: Yes, Miss Moffat.

> *They retire meekly through the study.* MISS MOFFAT *is alone. She looks at her watch; her armour loosens perceptibly; she is on edge and apprehensive. She goes towards the stairs, but before she reaches them, the garden door opens suddenly, and* MORGAN *appears. He wears a new dark suit, carries a travelling bag and his cap and looks dusty and tired. His manner is excited and unstable; he is alternately eager and intensely depressed. She stares at him, not daring to speak.*

MORGAN: I caught the early train. I knew they would all be watching for me, so I got out at Llanmorfedd and got a lift to Gwaenygam.

MISS MOFFAT (*fearfully*): Does that mean——

MORGAN: Oh, no news.

> *He puts down his bag and cap next to the armchair; she relaxes, comes down, and sits on the lower end of the sofa.*

MORGAN: Except that I am not hopeful.

MISS MOFFAT: Why not?

MORGAN (*sitting in the armchair*): They talked to me for one hour at the Viva——

MISS MOFFAT: That doesn't mean anything. Go on.

MORGAN: They jumped down hard on the New Testament question. As you said they would—you are very pale.

MISS MOFFAT: Better than a raging fever. Go on.

MORGAN: I spent five minutes explaining why Saint Paul sailed from a town three hundred miles inland.

MISS MOFFAT: Oh dear.

Their manner together has changed since we last saw them together; they are hardly at all teacher and pupil, superior and inferior, adult and child; they are more like two friends held solidly by a bond unsentimental and unself-conscious. MORGAN'S *English has immensely improved, and he expresses himself with ease.*

MISS MOFFAT: Parnell?

MORGAN: Parnell . . . Oh yes—I was going to stick up for the old chap, but when they started off with "that fellow Parnell", I told the tale against him for half an hour, I wasn't born a Welshman for nothing.

MISS MOFFAT: Ha . . . And the French?

MORGAN: Not good. I said "naturellement" to everything, but it didn't fit every time.

MISS MOFFAT: And the Greek verbs?

MORGAN: They were sarcastic.

MISS MOFFAT: Did the President send for you?

MORGAN: I had half an hour with him——

MISS MOFFAT: You did?

MORGAN: Yes, but so did the other nine candidates! He was a very kind and grand old gentleman sitting in a drawing-room the size of Penlan Town Hall. I talked about religion, the same as you said——

MISS MOFFAT (*correcting him, mechanically*): Just as you advised——

MORGAN: Just as you advised. He asked me if I had ever had strong drink, and I looked him straight in the eye and said "No".

MISS MOFFAT: Oh!

MORGAN: I was terrible—terribly nervous. My collar stud flew off, and I had to hold on to my collar with one hand, and he did not seem impressed with me at all. . . . He was very curious about you. Did you know there was an article in the *Morning Post* about the school?

MISS MOFFAT (*waving aside the news*): Was there? . . . But what else makes you despondent?

MORGAN: The other candidates. They appeared to me brilliant —I had never thought they would be, somehow! Two from Eton and one from Harrow, one of them very rich. I had never thought a scholarship man might be rich. He had his own servant.

MISS MOFFAT: Gosh!

MORGAN: And the servant looked so like my father I thought it was at first . . . And as I was leaving the examiners appeared to be sorry for me in some way, and I received the impression that I had failed. I——

He is suddenly depressed, rises and wanders towards the stairs. She catches his mood.

MISS MOFFAT: When shall we know?

MORGAN: The day after to-morrow. They are writing to you.

MISS MOFFAT (*rising and pacing towards the desk*): The villagers are all in their best, and talking about a holiday to-morrow. It is very stupid of them, because if you have failed it will make you still more sick at heart——

MORGAN: If I have failed? (*In sudden desperation.*) Don't speak about it!

MISS MOFFAT (*turning to him, surprised*): But we must! You faced the idea the day you left for Oxford——

MORGAN: I know, but I have *been* to Oxford, and come back, since then! (*Sitting on the lower end of the sofa, facing her.*) I have come back—from the world! Since the day I was born, I have been a prisoner behind a stone wall, and now somebody has given me a leg-up to have a look at the other side . . . (*vehement*) . . . they cannot drag me back again, they cannot, they *must* give me a push and send me over!

MISS MOFFAT (*sitting beside him, half-touched, half-amused*): I've never heard you talk so much since I've known you.

MORGAN: That is just it! I *can* talk, now! The three days I have been there, I have been talking my head off!

MISS MOFFAT: Ha! If three days at Oxford can do that to you, what would you be like at the end of three years?

MORGAN: That s just it again—it would be everything I need, everything! Starling and I spent three hours one night discussin' the law—Starling, you know, the brilliant one. . . . The words came pouring out of me—all the words that I had learnt and written down and never spoken—I suppose I was talking nonsense, but I was at least holding a conversation! I suddenly realised that I had never done it before—I had never been *able* to do it. (*With a strong Welsh accent.*) "How are you, Morgan? Nice day, Mr. Jones! Not bad for the harvest!"—a vocabulary of twenty words; all the thoughts that you have given to me were being stored away as if they were always going to be useless—locked up and rotting away—a lot of questions with nobody to answer them, a lot of statements with nobody to contradict them . . . and there I was with Starling, nineteen to the dozen (*Suddenly quieter.*) I came out of his rooms that night, and I walked down the High. That's their High Street, you know.

MISS MOFFAT (*nodding, drinking in the torrent with the most intense pleasure*): Yes, yes . . .

MORGAN (*looking before him*): I looked up, and there was a moon behind Magd—Maudlin. Not the same moon I have seen over the Nant, a different face altogether. Everybody seemed to be walking very fast, with their gowns on, in the moonlight; the bells were ringing, and I was walking faster than anybody and I felt—well, the same as on the rum in the old days!

MISS MOFFAT: Go on.

MORGAN: All of a sudden, with one big rush, against that moon, and against that High Street . . . I saw this room; you and me sitting here studying, and all those books—and everything I have ever learnt from those books, and from you, was lighted up—like a magic lantern—ancient Rome, Greece, Shakespeare, Carlyle, Milton . . . everything had a meaning, because I was in a new world—my world! And so it came to me why you worked like a slave to make me ready for this scholarship . . . (*Lamely.*) I've finished.

MISS MOFFAT (*smiling, dreamily*): I didn't want you to stop.

MORGAN: I had not been drinking.

MISS MOFFAT: I know.

MORGAN: I can talk to you too, now.

MISS MOFFAT: Yes. I'm glad.

THE SQUIRE *comes in from the front door, leaving it open behind him.* MORGAN *rises.*

THE SQUIRE (*coming down*): No sign of the feller-m -lad, dang it—Evans! There you are! . . . Well?

MORGAN: Good-day, sir, they are sending the result through the post.

THE SQUIRE: The devil they are. (*To* MISS MOFFAT, *as he sits in the armchair*). D'ye know I am finding this waiting a definite strain? . . .

MR. JONES *runs in from the study, in a state of excitement, as* MISS MOFFAT *rises and walks round the room.*

MR. JONES: Somebody said they had seen Morgan——

MORGAN: Day after to-morrow.

He sits, abruptly, on the settle.

MR. JONES: Oh . . .

He wanders sheepishly towards the open front door.

THE SQUIRE: Examiners all right, my boy?

MORGAN: Rather sticky, sir.

THE SQUIRE: Lot of old fogies, I expect. Miss Moffat, I told you you ought to have made inquiries at the other place. However . . .

MISS RONBERRY *runs in from the study, excited, carrying a sheet of music.*

MISS RONBERRY: Somebody said they had seen——

THE SQUIRE and MR. JONES (*in irritated chorus*): The day after to-morrow!

MISS RONBERRY (*dashed*): Oh . . . How are you, Morgan, dear . . .

MORGAN *half rises to greet her. She crosses to the desk.* MORGAN *looks thoughtfully before him.* MISS MOFFAT *tries to busy herself with a book at the dresser.*

MR. JONES (*wandering out into the porch*): The suspense is terrible.

THE SQUIRE: I know.

MR. JONES: Even the little children are worrying about——

He stops short; he has seen somebody coming down the village street; he looks again, doubtfully, starts, then peers anxiously into the room; everybody is preoccupied. He comes into the room, shuts the door, and stands a moment with his back to it.

MR. JONES: Morgan, my boy . . . are you not exhausted after your journey—would you not like something to eat?

MORGAN (*rousing himself from his thoughts*): I am rather hungry, yes——

MISS MOFFAT: But how stupid of me—Watty will boil you an egg—(*Moving towards the kitchen.*)—come along——

MORGAN (*rising*): Thank you—(*To the others.*)—excuse me——

MISS MOFFAT (*as she goes into the kitchen*): Did they spot the Dryden howler?

MORGAN (*following her*): No.

MR. JONES *crosses quickly and shuts the door after them.*

THE SQUIRE: You seemed very anxious to get 'em out of the room. What's the matter——

The front door opens suddenly, and BESSIE walks in. She has completely changed; she might be ten years older. Her hair is up; she wears a cheaply smart costume, with a cape, and looks dazzlingly pretty in a loose opulent style. Her whole personality has blossomed.

A pause. They stare at her. She is perfectly self-possessed.

BESSIE: Hallo!

THE SQUIRE (*mechanically*): How d'ye do . . .

BESSIE: I'm very well indeed, thanks, and how are you, blooming?

Her accent is nearer the ladylike than it has been yet.

THE SQUIRE: Yes, thanks . . . (*To the others.*) What *is* this?

MISS RONBERRY: I really couldn't say . . . Good gracious, it's Bessie W——

BESSIE: Right first time. Hello, Miss Ronberry, how's geography, the world still goin' round in circles? Hello, Mr. Jones, flirty as ever?

She sits on the sofa, completely at home.

THE SQUIRE: And to what do we owe this honour?

BESSIE: Well, it's like this——

MR. JONES (*to MISS RONBERRY, desperately*): Miss Ronberry, will you please return to your class——

MISS RONBERRY (*agog, shutting the front door*): They are quite safe, I left Mary Davies in charge——

BESSIE (*to* MR. JONES): No you don't. We've had too many secrets as it is——

MR. JONES: Three days ago she sent money to you—did you not receive the letter——

BESSIE: Yes I did, and all the others, till I was sick of 'em.

THE SQUIRE: What *is* all this?

BESSIE (*taking off her cape*): Last week I was glancing through the *Mid-Wales Gazette*, and I'm here to congratulate a certain young gent in case he has won that scholarship.

MR. JONES: Oh!

MISS RONBERRY: But what has that got to do with you?

BESSIE: You see, Miss, it's like this——

MR. JONES (*in a last effort to stop her*): Don't say it—don'r say it!

BESSIE: Four weeks yesterday, I had a baby.

> *A pause.* MISS RONBERRY *and* THE SQUIRE *stare at her.* MR. JONES *gives a sigh of impotent despair.*

THE SQUIRE: You had a what?

BESSIE: A baby. Seven pounds thirteen ounces.

THE SQUIRE: Good God, how ghastly.

MR. JONES (*moving up, as* MISS RONBERRY *sinks into the desk chair*): It is a disgustin' subject and——

BESSIE: It isn't disgusting at all, if I had a wedding-ring you'd think it was sweet.

> MRS. WATTY *hurries in from the kitchen.*

MRS. WATTY: Morgan Evans's luggage. Excuse me, sir——

> *She crosses, picks up the bag and cap, and is about to take them back to the kitchen when she catches sight of* THE SQUIRE'S *serious face.*

MRS. WATTY: Oh! . . . (*Fearfully.*) Any news?

THE SQUIRE (*rising*): Well, yes . . .

> *He goes towards the front door, turning to watch the scene;* MRS. WATTY *looks from* MISS RONBERRY *to* BESSIE, *then back, not having recognised her daughter the first time.*

MRS WATTY: Bessie! (*Dropping what she is carrying, in her*

excitement.) My, you do look a dollymop! Excuse me, sir . . .

THE SQUIRE: Say anything you like——

MRS. WATTY: Where d'you get them bracelets?

BESSIE: Present.

MRS. WATTY: Oh, that's all right . . . Where 'ave you been, you madam?

BESSIE: Turnin' you into a granny.

MRS. WATTY: A gra . . . (*Delighted.*) Well, *fancy!*

  MISS MOFFAT *comes in from the kitchen.*

MISS MOFFAT (*calling back into the kitchen*): And I should try and have a sleep if I were you——

MRS. WATTY (*as* MISS MOFFAT *comes down and begins to go upstairs*): You could 'ave knocked me down with a feather!

BESSIE: Hello.

  MISS MOFFAT *stops short, turns and looks at her.*
I've just been telling them you-know-what.

  It is plain she is no longer afraid of MISS MOFFAT. *The latter looks from one to the other, helplessly.*

THE SQUIRE: And now I think it's time you told us who the fellow is. I am going to take drastic proceedings——

MRS. WATTY: That's right, dear—who is it——

BESSIE: Well, as a matter of fact——

MISS MOFFAT (*with a cry, coming down*): No! I'll pay you anything . . . anything!

BESSIE (*kindly*): It's no good, Miss. (*To the others, quickly.*) It's Morgan Evans.

  A pause. MISS MOFFAT *puts her clenched fist to her eyes in despair.*

THE SQUIRE: What!

MISS RONBERRY (*dazed*): I don't believe it . . .

MRS. WATTY (*really upset, to* MISS MOFFAT): Oh, ma'am . . .

MISS MOFFAT: I've been dreading this, for months. In a terrible way it's a relief.

BESSIE: Bamboozlin' me every week he was in the gutter!

MISS MOFFAT: Lies, all lies, and I was glad to be telling them——

MISS RONBERRY (*suddenly articulate*): I can't go on listening!

I can't bear it! (*Wringing her hands.*) It all comes of meddling with this teaching—she was in my class—what *would* Papa have said! (*Collapsing in the armchair.*) This horrible unnatural happening——

MISS MOFFAT (*exasperated beyond endurance*): Don't talk nonsense, it isn't horrible, and it isn't unnatural! On the contrary, it's nature giving civilisation a nasty tweak of the nose. All we can say is that she led him on, but even she was only obeying her instincts—what is at the bottom of the whole thing, actually, is my own crass stupidity for allowing not one jot for humanity. (*Clinging wearily to the banister.*) I should have tried to understand and forestall, instead of riding rough-shod like a mare with blinkers. Her own mother begged me not to bring her here in the first place—even the Squire gave me a hint—even *he* knew more about human nature than I did——

THE SQUIRE: I say, you know——

MISS MOFFAT: But I must do a little reforming, if you please, and this is where it has landed us. (*Sitting listlessly on the settle, her head turned away.*) The schoolmistress has learnt a lesson, but it's a little late now.

BESSIE (*rising*): Where is he?

MRS. WATTY (*defending the kitchen door, trying not to shout*): Over my dead body, my girl——

BESSIE (*standing with her back to the audience, hands on hips*): She's right, mum, it's too late, I got a four weeks old baby, kickin' healthy and hungry, and I haven't got a husband to keep him, so his father's got to turn *into* my husband. That's only fair, isn't it?

THE SQUIRE: I'm sorry, Miss Moffat, but I'm inclined to agree——

BESSIE: I'll call him——

MR. JONES (*blinking*): There is no need to call him!

THE SQUIRE: What's the matter with you?

MR. JONES (*coming forward*): I am sorry to say that I have a strong feeling of affection for this young woman.

BESSIE (*sitting again on the sofa, amused*): Oh yes—I've got the face of an angel, haven't I?

MR. JONES: And I am willing to do my duty by rehabilitating

her in wedlock, and bestowing on the infant every advantage by bringing it up a Baptist.

MISS MOFFAT (*suddenly turning to him*): Are you serious?

MR. JONES: I am always serious.

MISS MOFFAT (*rising, to* BESSIE, *entreatingly*): I know it sounds cold-blooded, but . . . will you agree?

BESSIE: No, I won't. (*Good-humouredly.*) I don't want to hurt anybody's feelings, but I do draw the line.

MISS MOFFAT: Oh, please think again!

MRS. WATTY (*coming down round the sofa to* BESSIE): We're not pretendin' it's a windfall, but for a girl who's took the wrong turnin' it's a present! And you'd 'ave your own way in everything —wouldn't she, sir?

MR. JONES (*eagerly*): Of course——

MISS MOFFAT: Watty's put it perfectly . . . (*Sitting beside* BESSIE *on the sofa.*) I can't expect you to realise how much this means to me . . . except that I'm begging you, and begging doesn't come easily to me . . Will you?

BESSIE: I'd like to oblige . . . (*Looking at* MR. JONES *and giggling in spite of herself.*) . . . but really I couldn't! (*As he retreats despondently.*) Besides, my friend would be furious.

MRS. WATTY (*clutching at straws*): Your friend?

BESSIE: Ever such a nice gentleman, sporting, quite a swell, owns a racecourse. (*Catching her mother's eye.*) You needn't look like that, I only met him ten weeks ago. I'd started servin' behind a bar for fun, I was the picture of health and ever so lucky in the counter bein' very high.

THE SQUIRE: I have never heard such a conversation outside a police-court. I am seeking the safety of my own quarters— anything I can do, Miss Moffat——

He goes towards the front door.

BESSIE (*to him*): I suppose *you* wouldn't care to stake a claim?

THE SQUIRE: Good gracious——

He gives her a startled look and goes.

MISS MOFFAT: Doesn't this man of yours want to marry you?

BESSIE: 'E won't talk of anything else, but he won't have the baby. He says it would be different if the father'd been a pal of his—you can understand it, really, can't you? So I've got to give up my friend and marry Morgan Evans. (*As* MISS MOFFAT *rises and moves despairingly up to the bay window.*) Pity, 'cos my friend worships me. Ever since I left he keeps on sending me telegrams. I just got two at the station, and I expect I'll get some more to-night, isn't it rich? Mr. Jones wouldn't consider the baby without me?

MISS RONBERRY: The baby without you! Your child! What about your—your mother-love?

BESSIE: I expect you'll think I'm a wicked girl, but d'you know, I haven't got any!

MISS RONBERRY: Oh, what a vile thing to say, vile——

BESSIE (*rising*): Now listen, dear . . . (*going to her*) . . . you're seeing this baby as if it was yours, aren't you—you'd think the world of it, wouldn't you?

MISS RONBERRY: It would mean everything to me . . . (*suddenly pathetic*) . . . my whole life . . .

BESSIE: I have a pretty near idea how old you are; well, my 'rithmetic was never very good, but quite a year or two ago you were twice as old as I am now. When I'm your age I'll love the idea of a baby, but life hasn't begun yet for me—I'm just getting a taste for it—what do *I* want with a baby?

MRS. WATTY: That's what we all want to know!

BESSIE: Yes, mum, but you know what it is——

MISS RONBERRY (*rising*): You're inhuman, that's what you are! To think you don't want it . . .

> *She is on the point of bursting into foolish tears, and runs into the study.*

BESSIE: I didn't mean to be nasty—but inhuman indeed! I didn't want the baby, nobody would have, but I was careful so it's be all right, and now it is all right I want it to have a good time—but *I* want a good time too! I *could* have left it on a doorstep, couldn't I? But I must see it's in good hands—(*turning up to* MISS MOFFAT.)—and that's why I've come to Morgan Evans.

MISS MOFFAT (*turning to her*): You want to make him marry you, on the chance he will become fond enough of the child

to ensure its future—(*her voice rising.*)—your conscience will
be clear and later you can go off on your own?

MRS. WATTY *tries to silence them, pointing to the kitchen.*

BESSIE: I shouldn't be surprised——

MISS MOFFAT: In the meantime, it's worth while to ruin a
boy on—on the threshold of——

BESSIE: I don't know anything about that, I'm sure. (*Calling.*)
Morgan!

MISS MOFFAT: Ssh! (*Intercepting her, desperately.*) Wait a minute,
wait . . . There may be a way out—there must be——

MRS. WATTY: Gawd bless us, ma'am—I got it!

MISS MOFFAT: What?

MRS. WATTY: Why can't you adopt it?

BESSIE *and* MR. JONES *stare from her to* MISS MOFFAT.

MISS MOFFAT (*turning away*): Don't be ridiculous.

MRS. WATTY: Would that do you, Bessie?

BESSIE (*impressed*): Well! I never thought . . .

MRS. WATTY: Would it, though?

BESSIE (*after consideration*): Yes, it would.

MISS MOFFAT (*really taken aback, for the first time*): It *would?*
. . . But . . . but what would *I* do with a baby? I—I don't
even know what they look like!

MRS. WATTY: They're lovely little things—now it's all
arranged——

MISS MOFFAT: But it would be fantastic——

BESSIE (*going up to her, eagerly*): Oh, do, please, it'd put *everything*
to rights! I would know the baby was safe, Morgan Evans need
never know a thing about it, I can marry my friend, and it will
all be beautiful! He might grow like his father and turn out quite
nice, and anyway I'm not really so bad, you know—and he's on
the bottle now—and I could give all the instructions before I
go—and you could have it straight away, see, because if it's going
I don't want to have it with me longer than I can help, see, because
I'd only start gettin' fond of it, see——

MRS. WATTY (*to* MISS MOFFAT): Come on, ma'am, you've been
pushin' us about for three years, now we'll give *you* a shovel

MISS MOFFAT: But it's mad—I tell you——

MRS. WATTY: Not as mad as takin' *me* in was, with my trouble! You've allus been like that, you might as well go on—where's that old gumption of yours?

MISS MOFFAT: But I was never meant to be a mother—I'm not like Miss Ronberry—why, *she* is the one to do it——

MR. JONES (*hastily*): She would never agree—we were discussin' Marged Hopkins going to the workhouse—and she said she could never hold with any child born like that.

MISS MOFFAT: Oh . . . I suppose it would worry some folk . . . But Watty, you're the grandmother, and surely you——

MRS. WATTY: Oh, I couldn't! I don't bear it no ill-will, but every penny I get goes to the Corpse. You're the one, dear, reelly you are.

MISS MOFFAT (*after thought, decisively*): Bessie Watty, do you mean that if I do not adopt this child, you——

BESSIE: I will have to tell Morgan Evans, and he will have to marry me, I swear that.

MISS MOFFAT: And do you swear that you would never let Morgan Evans know the truth?

BESSIE: I swear. If there are any questions, I'll say it was my friend's.

    A pause.

MISS MOFFAT: Then . . . (*Sitting in one of the desks.*) . . . I give in.

BESSIE (*elated*): That's lovely. My friend *will* be pleased. I'll pop back to the public-house for his telegram and send him a nice one back. (*Taking her cape from the sofa.*) Good-bye all, we'll arrange details later, shall we? (*Showing them a clasp on her cape.*) My friend gave me this buckle, isn't it nice? He offered me a tiny one, real, but I think the false is prettier, don't you?

MR. JONES (*as she turns to go*): Are you going to take up a life of sin?

BESSIE (*smiling*): I shouldn't be surprised. I'm only really meself with a lot of gentlemen round me, y'know, and a nice glass o' port will never come amiss, neither. (*To* MRS. WATTY.) That cold water didn't really do the trick, mum, did it? . . . (*To*

MISS MOFFAT, *serious for a moment*.) Good-bye . . . I only did
it to spite you, y'know.

MR. JONES: You are not fit to touch the hem of her garment.

BESSIE (*rounding on him, good-humouredly*): Oh yes, I am! Just
because she's read a lot o' books. Books, books! . . . (*Embracing
the room with a magnificent gesture*.) Look at 'em all! I got more
out of life at my age than she has out o' them all her days—and
I'll get a lot more yet! What d'you bet me?

She goes out by the front door.

MRS. WATTY (*shutting the door after her, with a deep sigh*): That's
settled . . .

The voices of children, in the barn; singing "Dacw'n-ghariad".

MR. JONES (*making for the study door*): For which we must be
truly thankful . . .

MORGAN *walks in quickly from the kitchen. He goes straight
to* MISS MOFFAT; *his face is white and shocked; they stare at him,
instinctively silent.*

MORGAN: I have been waiting for her to go.

MISS MOFFAT: Why?

MORGAN: The Squire just came in to see me.

MISS MOFFAT: The fool! The clumsy idiotic fool——

MORGAN: Then it's true! . . .

A pause. The singing stops in the barn.
(*Looking at the others mechanically*.) He thought I knew Then he
said it was for the best—that I ought to be told. . . . It is funny.
She and I, we do not know each other at all—it was a long time
ago, and I never thought again about it—and neither did she, I
know she didn't . . . and here we are . . . (*To* MISS MOFFAT,
dully.) It is funny, too, because if you and I had not made that
bad quarrel, it would never have happened. . . . It ought to
make me feel older . . . but I feel more—young than I have ever
done before . . . (*Almost collapsing, suddenly*.) Oh God, why
should this happen to me . . .

MISS MOFFAT: Steady . . .

MR. JONES: There is no need for you to upset yourself, my boy.
Miss Moffat is going to take care of—of——

MORGAN: What?

Miss Moffat: I am going to adopt it.

Morgan (*to* Miss Moffat, *his old truculent self emerging*): What in hell do you take me for?

Mr. Jones: Morgan, swearing! Be haru ti——

Morgan (*in a rage*): I will swear some more too, if people talk to me like that! (*To* Miss Moffat.) What do you take me for?

Mr. Jones: Then what would you like to do, my boy——

Morgan: What would I like to do? (*Getting more and more Welsh.*) It is not a question of what I would like to do, or what I might be allowed, but what I am *going* to do—what any fellow with any guts in him must do! (*Crossing, impetuously.*) I am going to marry her!

Miss Moffat (*with a cry*): I knew this would happen, I knew——

Morgan: What else is there, when I have made a fool of myself and of her, and of the poor—the poor—I am not going to talk about any of it to anybody, all I will say is that Bessie Watty and I are going to get married as soon as we can, and that is final!

He flings himself into the armchair, closing his eyes.

Miss Moffat (*crossing and sitting on the sofa, hopelessly*): I see.

A knock at the front door. Sarah *hurries in, agog with excitement. She runs to* Mrs. Watty.

Sarah: Bessie's telegram from her friend, they send it from Penlan—— (*to the others gleefully, as* Mrs. Watty *opens the envelope*)—I never seed one before!

Mrs. Watty (*sniffing*): Poor chap, 'e'll be disappointed again . . . (*Placing the telegram on* Miss Moffat's *lap.*) What does it say, ma'am? . . . (*As* Miss Moffat *does not move, a most tearfully.*) Read it, ma'am, take your mind off things. . . .

Miss Moffat *glances half-heartedly at the telegram. A pause. She looks up at* Morgan.

Miss Moffat: You have won the scholarship. (*Reading.*) "First, Evans, Second Fayver-Iles, Third Starling. Congratulations."

Sarah *claps her hands and runs out by the front door.* Morgan *laughs bitterly and turns away.*

(*Folding up the telegram carefully, tucking it into her belt, still quiet, burning with a slow-mounting and deliberate fever.*) Lock the school door, Watty, will you?

MRS. WATTY (*to* MR. JONES, *tremulously*): Go in there, sir, I'll make you a cup of tea. . . .

>   MR. JONES *goes into the kitchen.* MRS. WATTY *locks the study door and follows him.*

MISS MOFFAT: Look at me, Morgan.

>   MORGAN: *faces her in the armchair, defiantly.*

For the first time, we are together. Our hearts are face to face, naked and unashamed, because there's no time to lose, my boy; the clock is ticking and there's no time to lose. If ever anybody has been at the crossroads, you are now——

MORGAN (*rising, and pacing restlessly up to the side window*): It is no good. I am going to marry her.

MISS MOFFAT: And I am going to speak to you very simply. I want you to change suddenly from a boy to a man. I understand that this is a great shock to you, but I want you to throw off this passionate obstinacy to do the right thing, which is natural at your age, and try to assume the sober judgment of somebody more *my* age. . . . Did you promise her marriage?

MORGAN: No, never——

MISS MOFFAT: Did you even tell her that you were in love with her?

MORGAN (*repelled*): No, never——

MISS MOFFAT: Then your situation now is the purest accident; it is to be regretted, but it has happened before and it will happen again. So cheer up, you are not the central figure of such a tragedy as you think——

MORGAN: That does not alter the fact that I have a duty to— to them both——

MISS MOFFAT: She has her own plans, and she doesn't want the child; and I am willing to look after it if you behave as I want you to behave. If you marry her, you know what will happen, don't you? You will go back to the mine. In a year she will have left you—both. You will be drinking again, and this time you will not stop. And you will enjoy being this besotted and

93

uncouth village genius who once showed such promise; but it will not be worth it, you know.

MORGAN (*moving to her, fighting*): There is a child, living and breathing on this earth, and living and breathing because of me——

MISS MOFFAT (*turning on him, with her old snap*): I don't care if there are fifty children on this earth because of you! . . . (*As he sits again, wearily in the armchair*). You mentioned the word "duty" did you? Yes, you have a duty, but it is not to this loose little lady, or to her offspring either.

MORGAN: You mean a duty to you?

MISS MOFFAT (*shaking her head, with a smile*): No. (*As he looks at her, arrested.*) A year ago I should have said a duty to me, yes; but that night you showed your teeth . . . you gave me a lot to think about, you know. You caught me unawares, and I gave you the worst possible answer back; I turned sorry for myself and taunted you with ingratitude. I was a dolt not to realise that a debt of gratitude is the most humiliating debt of all, and that a little show of affection would have wiped it out. I offer that affection to you, to-day.

MORGAN: Why are you saying this to me now?

MISS MOFFAT: Because, as the moments are passing, and I am going to get my way, I know that I am never going to see you again.

   A pause.

MORGAN (*incredulously*): Never again? (*Rising.*) But why?

MISS MOFFAT: If you are not to marry her, it would be madness for you to come into contact with the child; so if I am adopting the child, you can never come to see me; it is common sense. Actually there is no reason why you should ever come to Glansarno again; you have been given the push over the wall that you asked for, and you have grown out of this already.

MORGAN: But you . . . will be staying here—how can I never come back—after everything you have done for me?

MISS MOFFAT (*after a pause, smiling*): D'you remember, the last six months, I've gone for a long walk over Moel Hiraeth, every morning at eight, like clock-work, for my health?

MORGAN (*sitting*): Yes?

94

MISS MOFFAT: There's one bit of the road, round a boulder—
and there's an oak-tree, and under it the valley suddenly drops
sheer. Every morning regularly, as I was turning that corner, by
some trick of the mind, I found myself thinking of you working for
this scholarship, and winning it. And I experienced something
which must after all be comparatively rare: a feeling . . . of
complete happiness.

> *She is suddenly moved. He looks away slowly. She recovers.*

I shall experience it again.   No, Morgan Evans, you have
no duty to me. Your only duty—is to the world.

MORGAN (*turning to her*): To the world?

MISS MOFFAT: Now you are going, there is no harm in telling
you something. I don't think you realise quite how exceptional
you are, or what your future can become if you give it the chance.
I have always been very definite about the things I wanted, and
I have always had everything worked out to a T—p'raps that's
the trouble with me, I dunno. . . . I've got *you* worked out,
and it's up to you whether it will come right or not——

MORGAN (*eagerly*): Go on.

MISS MOFFAT: I rather made out to the Squire that I wanted
you to be a writer—the truth might have sounded ridiculous; but
stranger things have happened. You have brains, shrewdness,
eloquence, imagination and enough personality; and Oxford will
give you enough of the graces.

MORGAN: For what?

MISS MOFFAT (*simply*): Enough to become a great statesman
of our country. (*After a pause, as he stares at her.*) It needn't be
just politics—it could be more, much, much more—it could
be . . . for a future nation to be proud of. . . . P'raps I'm mad,
I dunno. We'll see. I know you're absurdly young for such an
idea, and that so far you've only got the groundwork—I know
all that; but I've got the measure of your intellect better than you
have yourself. It's up to you . . . (*After a pause.*) And now
doesn't Bessie Watty and her baby seem a little unimportant?

> *She hangs on his answer. A pause. He is looking straight
> before him.*

MORGAN (*quietly*): Yes.

MR. JONES *appears timidly from the kitchen.*

MR. JONES: Is it all right to ring the bell to say holiday to-morrow?

MISS MOFFAT: Yes.

MR. JONES'S *face lights up; he hurries to the study door, unlocks it, and disappears.*

MISS MOFFAT (*rising, suddenly*): I think that's all.

She goes to the back of the sofa and picks up MORGAN'S *bag and cap.*

MORGAN (*rising, and facing her*): But—I—I do not know what to say.

MISS MOFFAT (*smiling*): Then don't say it.

MORGAN (*looking round*): I have been . . . so much time in this room.

MISS MOFFAT: And the lessons are over.

MORGAN (*turning to her, impulsively*): I shall—always remember.

MISS MOFFAT (*shaking her head, with a smile*): Will you? Well, I'm glad you think you will.

She presses the bag and cap into his unwilling hands. IDWAL *runs in from the study, very excited.*

IDWAL: Please Miss Moffat, the band is out, and they say Morgan got to come down to Penlan Town Hall for Wales to see a real toff!

ROBBART *appears behind him.*

MORGAN (*unwillingly*): Na, ddim diolch——

ROBBART: Tyd, man, tyd, they never forgive you! (*An after-thought.*) And please Miss Moffat, Mr. Jones say is he to say school day after to-morrow, nine o'clock same as usual?

MISS MOFFAT (*turning to him, slowly*): Nine o'clock. The same as usual . . .

ROBBART: Yes, Miss Moffat.

He runs back into the study, followed by IDWAL. MISS MOFFAT *holds out her hand, smiling.*

MISS MOFFAT: Good-bye.

They shake hands. MORGAN *is too near tears to speak.*

MISS MOFFAT: And I had my heart set on coming up to London and having tea on the Terrace.

IDWAL (*putting his head round the barn door, and disappearing again*): Brysia, Morgan Evans, brysia!

> MORGAN *tries to say something, fails, and hurries into the study. As he shuts the door, the kitchen door opens, and* MRS. WATTY *appears cautiously.*

MRS. WATTY (*whispering*): Has he gone?

MISS MOFFAT: Yes. (*Crossing to the desk.*) It's all over.

MRS. WATTY: Oh no it isn't all over, ma'am! Because you're wanted in the kitchen—Bessie's sent a gentleman over to see you from the public-house——

MISS MOFFAT: Tell him I can't see anybody——

MRS. WATTY: 'E wouldn't understand, ma'am; you see, he's only four weeks old.

> MISS MOFFAT *turns and looks at her. A pause.*

MISS MOFFAT (*quietly*): I had forgotten—all about that.

MRS. WATTY: Poor little feller, nobody wants 'im! (*In a conspiratorial whisper.*) I only hope nobody'll put two and two together, ma'am, 'e's the spit of 'is father! (*Pressing a paper into her hand.*) This is 'is birth certificate she sent over . . . (*moving to the kitchen door*) . . . and I got everything else in there, and I'll see to the bottle. (*As* MISS MOFFAT *does not move.*) Come on, ma'am, you got to start some time!

MISS MOFFAT: Just coming.

> MRS. WATTY *goes into the kitchen. The sound of the village people singing and cheering down the road. A pause.*
>
> MISS MOFFAT *looks down at the birth certificate. The singing and cheering die down. A pause.*

MISS MOFFAT: Moffat my girl, you mustn't be clumsy this time. You mustn't be clumsy. . . .

> *The school bell begins to ring, clear and confident. She looks up, as she did once before, listening, smiling faintly. A vociferous burst of cheering in the village. She turns and walks towards the kitchen.*

CURTAIN